HER ALLIES

A Practical Toolkit
to **Help Men Lead**
Through Advocacy

HIRA ALI

T0284648

NEEM TREE
PRESS

Published by Neem Tree Press Limited 2021

95A Ridgmount Gardens London, UK WC1E 7AZ

info@neemtreepress.com

ISBN 978-1-91107-47-7 Paperback

ISBN 978-1-91107-48-4 Ebook

A catalogue record for this book is available from the British Library

Printed and bound in Great Britain by Biddles Limited

DEDICATION

This book is dedicated to my very own male allies who have provided unconditional support throughout various phases of my life: my grandfather who inspired me to dream big; my father who cherished me and passed on invaluable leadership lessons that have significantly impacted my personal and professional life; my brother who has helped me navigate male-dominated spaces with dignity and grace; my son who keeps me motivated and energised; and last but not the least—the man to whom I owe the most, especially in terms of my career trajectory—my husband, who has always been my greatest and truest ally in every sense of the word.

ACKNOWLEDGEMENTS

The years 2020 to 2021 have been very challenging for all of us. I couldn't have survived it without my family's support, especially my mother who keeps me grounded, grateful and resilient, even in the most trying times. I am also grateful to my friends, whose humour and generous listening pulled me through difficult times; my followers whose encouraging reviews kept me going; my team members who helped me create incredible projects; our clients who trusted us to deliver engagements; and my mentors for championing my work and providing referrals. A big, heartfelt thank you to all those who published my articles; featured my interviews; supported my initiatives; gave me shout-outs and brilliant reviews; invited me to talk on TV and radio shows, conferences and panel discussions; nominated me for awards and showcased my work throughout the year.

And finally, special thanks to Archna Sharma, Helen Lewis and especially Liz Buckley for their valuable support in turning this book into a reality. I am also very grateful to Barry Boffy, Marie Sola and Jiten Patel for their valuable insights that helped me in polishing the content of this book.

EARLY PRAISE FOR HER ALLIES

With *Her Allies*, Hira Ali has delivered the much-anticipated sequel to her ground-breaking book, *Her Way To The Top*. This new toolkit is a concise and practical guide for any man who wants to truly show up as a co-conspirator and collaborator with women to foster genuine gender equity in the workplace. Men who are ready to embark on the journey toward better allyship will find this guide jam-packed with gender intelligence and actionable strategies for transforming their good intentions into meaningful action. Two enthusiastic thumbs up!

W. Brad Johnson PhD
Professor of Psychology, US Naval Academy and
David G. Smith PhD
Associate Professor of Sociology, U.S. Naval War College.
Authors of *Athena Rising: How and Why Men Should Mentor Women and Good Guys: How Men Can Become Better Allies for Women in the Workplace*

Many of us have good intentions about wanting to challenge inequalities. We often want to do the right thing and to make a real difference, but when the task at hand seems that little bit too overwhelming for just one person to achieve, where do we find the tools to even start?

In *Her Allies*, Hira Ali has created a practical, step-by-step guide that not only explains the benefits of gender advocacy, but clearly outlines some of the practical ways that this can be achieved. This is a guide for men of all ages, backgrounds and industries, but remains an equally important reminder to women that they are as valuable an advocate for gender equality as their male allies. As an inclusion and diversity professional, I'm often looking for new and innovative ways to encourage others to challenge the status quo and in this book, I have found a clear and practical tool to assist me.

Barry Boffy
Head of Inclusion and Diversity, British Transport Police

So many books identify the problems of gender inequality, but this book actually lets you know how to address those problems in a practical and meaningful way. Ditch your excuses of worrying that you'll say the wrong thing, not being clear on the issues, or not knowing how. The pragmatic step-by-step approaches that Hira Ali shares are all you need to take action as an ally to women inside and outside of the workplace. This book has the potential to halve the time it will take us to get to gender parity globally. It's compulsory reading for every man who wants a fairer world, where we can all thrive.

Jenny Garrett OBE
Founder, Executive Coach and Leadership Trainer

I am a big fan of Hira and her writing. From her myriad articles supporting women's issues, leadership, diversity and inclusion, to her books; I always come away appreciating her writing style and the information she imparts. *Her Allies* is especially impactful, in my opinion, as it addresses men directly in a straightforward and informative manner. The first step in addressing an issue is to realise there is an issue and then become informed about it. *Her Allies* does just that. There is no judgment or blaming. Rather, it is full of well-documented information meant to educate and inform men about gender stereotypes in the workplace. Much of which can easily be disregarded and overlooked if everything remains status quo. There are also useful tips and suggestions for creating a more inclusive environment. This is not only good for employee morale, it is also good for a company's bottom line. My hope is that men in positions, and in the right mindset to become our allies, will take time to read this book and put some thought into how it may apply to them and/or their businesses.

Marie Sola

President and Founder, Daughters of Change

On your journey into allyship, Ali's book is an essential primer. It makes no assumptions about what you know or don't know. It provides indispensable background context and then takes you into the *how* of allyship. While the author speaks primarily to men being allies for women, many of the principles are just as valid to other forms of allyship. I would recommend it whether you are a woman, a man or a gender diverse leader.

Jiten Patel ACIB

Conscious Inclusion Thought Leader, C-Suite Inclusive Leadership Coach, and Author of Demystifying Diversity.

Allyship is an important way of showing support for others, but the question of how to be an effective ally isn't always a simple or straightforward one. This book provides good, practical steps for male allies to take when looking at gender equality, be it at home or in the workplace, and it will hopefully give men the confidence to become better allies in general. A must read for men everywhere.

Jasvir Singh OBE

Barrister, Chair of City Sikhs, Member Of Mayor of London's Commission for Diversity in the Public Realm

A practical, solid and enlightening guide that details everyday actions allies can take to support women at work and in communities. Hira has provided valuable insights and actionable ideas to take the next step in being an inclusive leader and ally. This book is an important resource for everyone who is willing to make a positive difference.

Afzal Khan CBE
Member of UK Parliament

Hira Ali shares proven research with tangible tools and talk tracks to have a more productive conversation about gender inclusion in the workplace. Every ally could benefit from reading this!

Julie Kratz (she/her)
Pivot Point CEO and Founder

The answer to most of life's ills rests with the men who cause them. This book is an exceptionally accessible tool for men to begin to address them. Essential reading.

Nazir Afzal OBE
Former Chief Prosecutor, NW England

For all those with the right intentions, here is a guide that will help you become an advocate. It is full of practical steps we can take in creating organisations we'd love our children to work in.

Gavin Stephens
Chief Constable, Surrey Police Headquarters

Having been in the Diversity and Inclusion field for over 17 years, there aren't many books that have grabbed my attention from the word go, however *Her Allies* is a really informative and practical book, ideal for anyone looking to pick up tips on how to be a supportive ally. Covering topics including making assumptions, stereotyping and generalising, I found this book and its contents really useful. It is a must for anyone wanting to become an ally for gender equality. I particularly enjoyed the section around acknowledging your bias. Congratulations Hira, on a fantastic piece of work!

Paul Sesay
I CEO/Founder I Inclusive Companies Limited

There are many men out there who want to do more and have no idea where or how to start for fear of getting it wrong. *Her Allies* is the perfect first step for men willing to listen, to challenge themselves and other men, but more importantly a willingness to take action.

Nathan Ashley
Senior Public Policy Manager at Voi Technology

Hira Ali does it again! Another must have book. *Her Allies* offers practical suggestions in a truly engaging way; the structure and layout is spot on, encouraging the reader to learn to challenge themselves before moving on to challenge others and the system at large! Absolute must-read for anyone who wants to change their culture for good!

Vanessa Vallely OBE
Managing Director, WeAreTheCity

Her Allies is an important contribution to the effort to get men positively engaged in the need for a more inclusive workplace and society. Essential reading for everyone who wants to make a difference.

Mark Wild
Chief Executive Officer at Crossrail Ltd

In reading Hira's book, I was reminded that EVERYONE should read this book. Hira shares an abundance of tools to be a better ally versus simply statistics. *Her Allies* is not about shaming men, it is about illuminating them (you don't know what you don't know). Hira is quick to point out that privilege does not mean men haven't struggled, simply the struggles are vastly different from women, and women of colour. This book is insightful, educational, and most important, truthful. As men strive to be better equipped to be a better ally, they need look no further than, *Her Allies*. Kudos, Hira!

Nicki Anderson
Director of Women's Leadership Program—L.E.A.D.S, Benedictine University

If you're thinking of reading this book then you are acknowledging that there is a need for personal change. Her Allies provides practical ways for men to rethink mental obstacles that create barriers to equality and inclusivity. This simple thought provoking book goes beyond encouraging you to be become an advocate, it challenges you to operate with courage and determination to become the change agent that leads the way.

Wasim Khan MBE
Chief Executive, Pakistan Cricket Board

TABLE OF CONTENTS

BACKGROUND—HOW IT ALL STARTED

After the release of my first book, *Her Way To The Top*, I was invited to various organisations to deliver book talks and workshops to discuss the internal and external challenges holding women back from smashing the glass ceiling. On several occasions, I was asked what others could do to support women's career advancement. During these sessions I would often meet well-intentioned men who were keen to support women in their circle but were unsure where to start. To facilitate these allies, I wrote a *Forbes* article for International Men's Day in 2019. My article was well received; Isabelle Magyar, Global Advisor for HeForSheInitiative at United Nations Women even shared it with the program team and champions. Following the success of that article, friends and colleagues encouraged me to further explore this topic and share my perspective.

At my book launch anniversary in March 2020, right before the world entered the pandemic, we conducted a live poll on the *Factors Most Impacting A Woman's Climb To The Top*, followed by an interactive panel discussion on the topic of *Her Allies*—where we discussed the role of government legislation and policies, media, organisations and male allies—in smashing the glass ceiling. Thirty percent of the female poll participants agreed that male allies had a direct impact on their career. The panel discussion was attended by leading Diversity and Inclusion (D&I) champions from the public and private sector and facilitated by my dear friend and business partner Cherron Inko-Tariah MBE, who is founder of The Power of Staff Networks. Other panellists included Barry Boffy from The British Transport Police, Coleen Andrews from the Cabinet Office, Neville Gaunt from Mind Fit, Emma Ko from the Women's Equality Party and Anne-Marie Headley from Workforce Buddy.

After half an hour, we all agreed that we needed a full day event on this topic, which the British Transport Police graciously agreed to host.

Factors Impacting a Woman's climb to the Top
Her Allies Panel Discussion held on March 4th 2020

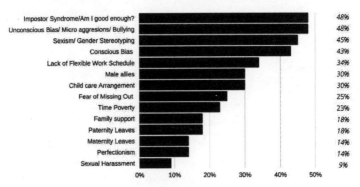

One of the panel discussions, *Role of Organisations in Supporting a Woman's Climb to the Top*, led by a wonderfully supportive ally and D&I head of British Transport Police, Barry Boffy, started the conversation with this question, 'When we talk about an organisation, what exactly do we mean? What are we referring to?' Barry and the group concluded, 'An organisation in and of itself is not a sentient being with thoughts, values or priorities of its own, so it's important to remember that point and not to assign any blame for a toxic or exclusionary culture to what is essentially an abstract concept. Psychologically speaking, when we depersonalise an organisation in this way it makes it impossible for us to challenge the status quo. It moves to the "too difficult" pile. We can't change an "organisation" (it becomes a David versus Goliath battle) but what we can do is influence and change the people that sit at the heart of this organisation. It pays to remember that an organisation is only as good as the people at its heart.'

In trying to define this, one of the delegates suggested that an organisation is ultimately a 'collection of individuals with a shared goal or purpose,' which brought the focus of the discussions back around to the term 'individuals' and who ultimately holds the power in organisational change, focus or activity: the people at its heart.

All organisations are composed of individuals with their own beliefs, values and priorities which, in turn, influence organisational beliefs, values and priorities. To affect real change, you must appeal to the individuals within an organisation who can drive that change. This discussion was a defining moment that triggered the concept of this book; *Her Allies* is about those steps we can all take as individuals to make a difference for society as a whole.

Meanwhile, in the exact same year, a horrific motorway rape incident in my home country of Pakistan sparked a nationwide fury and a gamut of emotions ranging from disgust and frustration to anger and despondency. This bone-chilling incident begged the question—how can we eradicate such horrific vices from society? Rape is a heinous crime that leaves lasting psychological scars on its victims. Yet, rape conviction rates are appallingly low—not just in Asia—but in countries including the US and UK. An extreme example of gender violence, rape is a by-product of a flawed patriarchal society that embeds deeply intertwined issues including sexism, toxic masculinity, flawed gender norms, systemic bias, ignorance, unequal power play, exploitation of the weak and vulnerable, peer pressure and entitlement. In some places, it also involves corruption, bribery and religious misconception. Although rape may not be common in the workplace, sexual harassment is still rampant and one of the major external challenges negatively impacting women at work. According to a report by TUC, one in two women and two in three LGBTQI+ workers experience sexual harassment in the workplace. And then there are other less evil but equally debilitating vices such as micro-aggressions, systemic inequality and harmful stereotyping or labelling that routinely deter women in the public and private space.

The motorway rape incident prompted me to formally launch the #HerAllies campaign under the banner of my organisation– International Women Empowerment events. The campaign aimed to create awareness and positive dialogue while exploring the role of organisations, religious bodies, government, media and *Her Allies* (men and women) in overcoming barriers women regularly face in their personal and professional lives. The basis of the campaign was a three-page manifesto which outlined numerous actions you can take as #HerAllies. Many of these responsibilities were based on the job description my team and I had created for male ambassadors appointed for our 2019 Women Empowerment Conference in the Maldives. The manifesto aimed to answer this question, 'how do we help fight a culture that breeds these harmful gendered practices?' Most men who joined the campaign acknowledged that for too long women have suffered within a gendered social and cultural environment that engages in blame games and fails to take responsibility; it is time to change the narrative. But few actually knew how to translate this awareness into actionable results. I was thrilled when hundreds of people pledged to join our #HerAllies campaign.

In late 2020, the bold and inspiring Eesha Afridi invited me to attend *Pakistani Youth Lean In Circle* where the discussion focused on gender neutral practices. Dozens of students from various educational institutions attended the Zoom meeting with a common goal to identify how they could personally advance gender equality. That discussion gave me immense hope and reaffirmed the need for a toolkit or guide delineating simple, everyday actions we all can take to play our part. Finally, repeated lockdowns due to the pandemic allowed me to channel the distress and uncertainty into something productive. . . and lo and behold, *Her Allies* took shape!

GETTING THE MOST OUT OF THIS TOOLKIT

I am a huge fan of research and surveys. However, I wrote this book as a toolkit with less fluff and more action. I wanted to address both basic and advanced issues, given my experience working across countries, cultures and genders. Over time, I have realised that nothing is too basic. In fact, I have been repeatedly surprised that a majority of people don't employ some of these very obvious actions detailed within. I have also realised that irrespective of our education, age, background and gender, we all have developed inherent biases over time. Let's face it—given how many of us were raised and conditioned, sometimes women have biases against other women too. Kristen Pressner's famous *TED Talk: Are You Biased?* was an eye-opener for me. In her talk, Kristen discloses how she has bias against women leaders even though, at first, she found it hard to believe, considering she is a leader herself (she works in human resources and encourages women to step up in their roles). She realised her own bias given how she responded to requests differently solely based on gender. She shares how she was approached by two team members asking her to have a look at their compensation. A few days later, as she was ironically researching unconscious bias, she discovered she had very different reactions to the same request given how she associated the word 'provider' with men.

Similarly, Boston-based writer Catherine Nichols, also experienced this first-hand. After finishing her novel, she sent a pitch to 50 literary agents, overwhelmingly female. She had just two positive replies. She then sent out exactly the same material to 50 more agents, but this time she used a male name and received 17 positive replies. Furthermore, she received constructive criticism on how to improve the novel, help she was never offered when she was writing under a woman's name. And this experience is not merely anecdotal; there are research studies that also support the argument that women can be biased against women. Vernā Myers, an inclusion strategist and cultural change catalyst, also shared her experience of boarding a plane and being thrilled that a female pilot was flying it because women entering the stratosphere prompted her excitement. However, when the plane started experiencing turbulence, she started questioning the female pilot's skill and wondering if the pilot was capable of flying the plane—a question she never had with a male pilot. Vernā realised that anxiety made her lean on a bias she never thought she had!

I am thankful to these thought leaders for being so open and vulnerable; hearing their stories made me realise that I have my own biases. From time to time, I have to check my own inherent biases and gender-blind spots; I still have not mastered the art of allyship. Although I am a woman, and a woman of colour at that, I am constantly learning and evolving.

I love the advice of Karen Catlin, author of *Better Allies*, who proposes that allyship is a journey during which you learn and improve as you go along. After deciding to write this book, I researched existing material on allyship. It took me some time to figure out how I could present the information in an easy-to-understand way that is relevant to my audience from different countries and cultures. I could best achieve this by building on Karen's journey metaphor; I am going to start with what you can do on your own and then move on to how you can challenge others, and ultimately, organisations and systems. Some of you may be new to this journey, while others may be halfway along or already in the final stages of adopting these approaches.

Please pardon me if I sound unintentionally patronising—the goal is to offer you effective strategies from a female perspective, but as a self-help toolkit, it includes a number of dos and don'ts, which may sound imposing. I sincerely hope you take it in the spirit with which it's intended—to help you become a better advocate. The last thing I want to do is to overwhelm and deter allies like you who have good intentions—you are among the 'good guys' as David Smith and Brad Johnson call them in their book by the same name. You are a man with your heart in the right place.

Though I do take pride in my feminism, I am aware that this female equality movement has earned itself a bad name over time and you may not support its stance. As powerful as this buzzword sounds, many people are oblivious to its actual connotations and have stigmatised it, even though the literal definition of feminism is 'the advocacy of women's rights on the grounds of political, social, and economic equality to men.'

The goal is to create a society in which an individual's gender does not restrict her from an equitable shot at success and happiness. Nothing more, nothing less. Feminists do not harbour any secret desires to propagate female supremacy, nor do they demand any special privileges for the latter. Feminists are not anti-men, nor are they anti-marriage. I have no reservations attributing many of my own successes to the supportive men in my life, be it my father, husband or brother. The whole point of feminism is only to demand equal rights for women in every sphere and walk of life. It is as simple as that. However, to engage the 'good guys' in our conversation, I will avoid this topic for now but not without highlighting how important it is for feminism to be trans inclusionary. It's not uncommon for transwomen and non-binary people to be victims of misogyny too. In the words of journalist Robin Dembroff, 'Those who enact misogyny often don't know or care what chromosomes someone has: they react to gender variance and nonconformity.'

That does beg the question—is this book mainly for men? I recognise that gender is about more than anatomy—it encompasses how individuals personally identify themselves. Many of the strategies offered in this book are addressed to allies that primarily identify as male. But, to be honest, as many early reviewers have highlighted, this book is for everyone, irrespective of gender, age, background, race or faith. It is written for those who aspire to be more gender-savvy, especially considering how women can have biases too. Moreover, at the stage we are in, we can never have enough allies, so if someone from outer space is willing to join the cause, I say: bring it on!

Driving societal change is never easy—cultural shifts do not happen overnight and that's why we need to actively campaign, build awareness and engage in uncomfortable conversations around recurrent themes with as many decision makers and influencers as we can, beginning first with family, friends and colleagues. Sarah Everards's disappearance and murder case, followed by the *Everyone's Invited* campaign, necessitates a massive change in the status quo. That change can begin with one person at a time—and that one person can be you. And me. And your friend. And my friend. And so on. How can we individually challenge stereotypes and change the narrative to collectively drive true change? This book is my answer to that critical question. Most of the strategies within pertain to women in the workplace, but they apply to all spaces where women participate. You don't have to be an influencer or a Human Resources lead or Diversity and Inclusion professional, nor do you necessarily need to engage in serious activism. You can start small, but taking that first step is critical, which is why I invite you to start with this book and be part of the conversation.

Hira Ali

INTRODUCTION

'And my advice to young men today: you are lucky guys because you have a chance to join the greatest revolution in human history, the gender equality revolution.'
-Michael Kaufman-

To truly promote equality, we cannot dismiss support from those who can potentially be our greatest allies—men! We need to encourage men to step up and play their part. And we need men to help us navigate a system and world primarily designed for them—a world where they largely remain a dominant force occupying powerful roles everywhere. If you are reading this right now with the goal to be more aware and intentional, thank you for your interest in, and commitment to, advancing gender equality. Let's begin by having a look at what allyship actually is.

WHAT IS AN ALLY?

Allyship has increasingly played a key role in supporting marginalised groups who are continuously short-changed by justice and equality.

Debra Meyerson and Megan Tompkin call allies *tempered radicals*—catalysts for change who challenge organisational structures that disadvantage women while remaining committed to the success of the organisation. During my previously mentioned book anniversary panel, participants arrived at the following definitions of allyship and allies:

1. Allies are individuals who provide sponsorship to women, champion them in rooms they are not in, give coaching feedback on their work and how they are showing up in the business, and help them raise their visibility.
2. Allies provide greater support to the company's D&I practitioners so their D&I work is elevated to the proper level and receives attention from the rest of the organisation, including middle management.
3. Allies commit to improving their own self-awareness so they can be a catalyst for change and become a role model for others.

Gill Whitty-Collins, author of *Why Men Are Winning at Work*, argues that until powerful men start to understand the problem and promote women equally, nothing will change. 'It's not about obvious sexism,' she writes. 'The conscious stuff is horrendous, but it's easier to deal with because it's just wrong. What's very difficult to tackle is the unconscious bias from well-intentioned men, who genuinely think they are promoting men for big jobs because they are better. Of course, that can be right 50 percent of the time but, based on the data, it cannot be right 95 percent of the time.'

It is not humanly possible to always be aware of other people's thoughts and expectations. After all, each person's map is different to yours. Their perceptions, perspectives and model of the world informs how they act and react. Each individual views the world through their own tinted perspective, which could be the same, or different, from yours. Authentic and active allies acknowledge this and know that while you can't understand all viewpoints, you can be open to learning, improving and changing by building self-awareness to foster fairness in everyday interactions, free from assumptions and biases. When you become an ally, you will embrace that allyship is a process, a journey of development and evolution.

Here it is important to make a distinction. Allies are not saviours, protectors or knights in shining armour who need to rescue women. While this may be true and appropriate in some situations, a large majority of women do not need saving or wish to be rescued. Hence, allies need to avoid appearing patronising, infantilising, condescending or worse—all-knowing. They need to work in complementary roles side-by-side as co-pilots, advocates, mentors, sponsors, defenders and amplifiers, who seek to level the playing field. Karen Catlin, author of *Better Allies*, notes the difference between allies and saviours: allies push for systemic change on a macro-level and not just one-off situations. They are on the lookout for major discrepancies that will impact a huge group of people versus just one. They challenge ingrained behaviours and remove equity barriers—not necessarily the easy way, but the right way, without shortcuts and without any desire to merely 'look' good. Quite simply, they avoid performative allyship.

BCG—Boston Consultant Group's worldwide data indicates that among companies where men are actively involved in gender diversity, 96 percent report progress. Conversely, among companies where men are not involved, only 30 percent show progress. The curated research report, *Men as Allies*, demonstrates that an enhanced understanding of the influential impact of male allies at work led many organisations to recognise men as critical allies in the diversity and inclusion equation. The Gloria Cordes Larson Center for Women and Business (CWB) at Bentley University explores what has fuelled the trend in its dedicated report. Some of these included people taking notice—as actress Emma Watson did when she addressed the United Nations in 2014—urging men to join the feminist movement under the banner #HeForShe. 'Gender equality is your issue too,' she told men as the UN Women Goodwill Ambassador. Launched in September 2014, #HeForShe is a movement that aims to inspire and encourage men to take action against gender inequality. Former President Obama garnered attention when he proclaimed he was a feminist and soon other male public figures and celebrities followed suit. In 2015, Justin Trudeau, Prime Minister of Canada, formed the first gender-balanced Cabinet. When asked why parity was important to him, he responded, 'Because it's 2015.' Notably, the Prime Minister of Spain, Pedro Sánchez, has built a cabinet in favour of women. Sadiq Khan, Mayor of London, also openly owns his feminist stance and has appointed Deputy Mayors of which half are women. In a letter, which he kindly addressed to me congratulating me on the publication of the first book, he wrote how it's unacceptable that gender can still play a role in how much you get paid and your career prospects. He added, '. . .to bring about the changes we want to see, men must play an active role, which is why my Our Time Program has male, as well as, female champions.'

Luckily, most men are already well aware of the impact of gender bias and the methodised sexism that women experience. They understand these negative effects from women in their circle and these very men are eager to dial-up inclusion efforts but they don't know where to start. If this resonates with you, then I have written this book for you. This allyship guide leverages your genuine proclivity to do better. It encourages you to venture into bold conversations and enter unchartered territories. It also equips you with gender intelligence that makes you an equality advocate both privately and publicly.

WHAT IS HOLDING YOU BACK?

University of Cambridge research, confirmed by the McKinsey/LeanIn.Org study, identified an 'Intention Gap' between intention and implementation. Many sources recognise that men generally have good intentions. However, when it comes to actually taking action, many fail to do so. Let us explore some reasons why men are hesitant to fully commit.

Whilst not true for all, or at all times, some people from the older generation may have stronger views about traditional hierarchies, hold more antiquated beliefs and show less awareness of gender equality, hence are more likely to hold a rigid perspective. However, the 2014 Pershing Harris Poll found that some younger men shared similar views to their older male counterparts. Younger men were less open to accepting women leaders than older men were.

A 2014 Harvard Business School (HBS) survey of MBA graduates showed that half of the men expected their own careers to take precedence over their partners. Likewise, two-thirds of their male peers believed their wives would handle childcare. This research dispels the notion that millennial men would be natural allies for women or view them as equals. The HBS MBA survey concluded, 'Indeed, this information raises a serious concern that unless something is done soon to change millennial men's attitudes toward women, these men ascending to the C-suite may hinder—rather than advance—current efforts to reduce the discriminatory effects of gender bias.' A 2016 study conducted by McKinsey and

LeanIn.Org further supported the thesis and concluded that at our current pace, 'it will take more than 100 years for the upper reaches of US corporations to achieve gender parity.'

Interview findings in Catalyst's Report: *Engaging Men in Gender Initiatives: What Change Agents Need to Know,* revealed three key barriers that could undermine men's support for initiatives to end gender bias: apathy, fear, and real or perceived ignorance of gender issues. Another deterrent is the notion that 'we've made progress and we are done.' This so-called 'ally fatigue' occurs when advocates become discouraged by slow progress.

Apathy
Interviewees did not find a compelling reason to become actively involved in gender initiatives, perhaps because men are often unaware of what they stand to gain by championing gender equality. According to *Good Guys,* when men hear something is a women's issue, they mentally tune out—not because they don't care—but because they assume it's for women. Framing equality discussions as women's issues gives men a free pass. When they hear the word gender, they often assume gender means 'for women.' They believe they have no psychological standing or ownership to support taking action.

Professor Paul Boyle, Vice-Chancellor, University of Leicester, UK was of the opinion that some men may not believe gender equality is their concern or a critical issue that warrants change. He notes that, 'In our institutions, gender equality discussions are dominated by women while men are getting on with research and other activities.'

Fear
Fear was a major factor too—fear of losing status was primary.

Respondents shared a zero-sum perspective that supporting women may somehow lead to diminished opportunities for themselves.

The second fear involved the fear of making mistakes. Men believed they would inadvertently expose themselves to criticism from women including what is called the 'Pedestal Effect.' This occurs when men receive special treatment and shout outs for even small acts of gender equality. This effect can be particularly exasperating for women who have shouldered years of emotional labour and carried the burden of equality. As Smith and Johnson aptly put it, 'women have done so with nary a man in sight.'

In the same study, men also believed that despite their good intentions, they would face intense scrutiny and women would consider them part of the problem versus part of the solution.

The report further revealed concerns corporate partners have heard:

- I have been trained as a man to think that I am the problem.
- I keep my head down. No matter what I say it could be misunderstood.
- If I make a comment, they will see me as 'the old white guy'. I might say something wrong, so I don't bring my full self to work.
- I worry I will be offensive. Sometimes I can't get my point across because I am being so careful.
- It could be career limiting to make a mistake.
- Merit will be compromised. We're lowering our standards to accept more women at higher levels who are not qualified.

Another study, published in the *Journal of Organisational Dynamics*, indicates that men are significantly more reluctant to interact with their female colleagues following the #MeToo movement.

Lastly, major deterrents included the natural fear of judgment, backlash and disapproval from male peers, also known as the dreaded 'wimp penalty.' Men are stigmatised through association with women's initiatives at work and often feel inhibited— not so much by women's judgments—but by that of their male counterparts. Men look to other men for affirmation of their masculinity; taking action against gender bias means potential loss of acceptance from male peers and a risk to their manhood.

Research shows that men experience social penalties, including rejection and loss of status—which are often harsher than those women face—when they deviate from their assigned gender scripts. And, to be honest, there is no surprise here as to why men would be cautious. We understand how hard this can be—we too, as women, have been bearing the brunt of societal judgment for as long as we can remember.

Yet another interesting observation is that while women's rights and empowerment have evolved over time, men have hardly matched pace with their idea of masculinity; that blueprint from decades ago is still intact even though the world looked very different then. Research suggests that organisational culture has a role to play in this—by rewarding strict conformity to masculine norms, organisations may inadvertently compromise their performance.

Engaging Men In Gender Initiatives: What Change Agents Need to Know is a valuable report that highlights four common masculine norms that are emphasised to varying degrees across cultures.

'Avoid all things feminine.'	'Be a winner.'
Perhaps *the* cardinal tenet of masculinity, this rule mandates that men should never be seen or acknowledge conforming to any feminine norms.	This principle concerns the attainment of status and thereby defines as manly any activity that increases men's wealth, social prestige, and power over others.
'Show no chinks in the armour.'	**'Be a man's man.'**
Men should be tough in both body and spirit. Physical toughness means never shrinking from the threat of physical harm; while displaying emotional toughness requires that men conceal such emotions as fear, sadness, nervousness, and uncertainty.	Also known as being 'one of the boys,' this rule of masculinity calls for men to win the respect and admiration of other men and to appear to enjoy a special sense of camaraderie with male peers. Being a man's man means visibly complying with all masculine norms.

Source: *Engaging Men in Gender Initiatives: What Change Agents Need To Know by Catalyst*

These men have chafed against the edges of this traditional, fixated ideology and its harmful norms. Tony Porter, author and activist, refers to this collective socialisation of men as the 'man box'. Most men have been unable to detach themselves from this pattern to form a new narrative.

Real or Perceived Ignorance of Gender Issues

Finally, the aforementioned research study by Catalyst also revealed that lack of awareness or ignorance was a critical barrier for men to support efforts of gender inequality. This contention is consistent with the finding that the less aware men were of gender bias, the less committed they were to issues of gender equality. Men who were more aware of gender bias were more likely to recognise the importance of achieving gender equality. Additional results reveal three key factors that predict a man's awareness of gender bias:

- Defiance of certain masculine norms.
- The presence or absence of women mentors.
- A sense of fair play.

Of these three factors, a strong sense of fair play, defined as a strong commitment to the ideals of fairness, was the primary differentiator for men who actively championed gender equality.

THE PERSONAL BENEFITS OF ALLYSHIP

Today, the movement for women's equality remains stymied, stalled. Women continue to experience discrimination in the public sphere. They collide against glass ceilings in the workplace, experience harassment and less-than-welcoming environments in every institution, miss out on career opportunities, face motherhood penalties and huge wage gaps, fight to control their own bodies, and struggle to end their victimisation through rape, domestic violence and trafficking.

Author of *How to Lead like an Ally*, Julie Kratz, notes that the workplace is built for men to succeed and workplace rules have been defined by men. She adds: 'Today's workplace still somewhat resembles 1950s-era Mad Men: plagued with sexual harassment, women toiling behind the scenes in low-paying positions, socially mandated after-hour activities, and rigid in-office hour requirements.'

In light of the above, one of the most obvious and compelling reasons to be an ally and push gender parity is that it's fair and democratic to do so. A McKinsey's *Women in the Workplace* report further reveals that women are not leaving the workplace to have children; they are leaving workplaces that fail to treat them fairly. That's a huge point of distinction. Allies can help change the downward spiral of this negative trend. To this point, minority men are often prominent and vocal allies for women, perhaps because their own experience contending with systemic workplace inequities provides insight on how traditional workplace rules shape behaviour and outcomes for women.

The Catalyst Research study indicates that many men feel more vested when they consider allyship to be a social responsibility—their participation can help improve the communities in which they operate. Those who display a strong sense of fairness are significantly more likely to become male advocates for gender equity. And then there are others who see what Consultant Chuck Shelton calls *Sustainable Collaborative Advantage*, when you are known as a man who collaborates well with women, women will choose to work with you.

Secondly, women have transformed the workplace and are here to stay. Almost half the labour force is female. Women have demonstrated the centrality of gender in social life; in the past two decades, gender has joined ranks with race and class as one of the three building blocks of identity around which social life is organised, and it only makes sense to improve how you work with this sizeable portion of the employed population.

Some of the world's most influential institutions including the World Bank, Goldman Sachs, the International Monetary Fund, Ernst and Young, the World Economic Forum, McKinsey & Company, and others, have published research that demonstrates increased competitiveness when women fully participate in the economy. As Robert Zoellick, former Director of the World Bank, notes, 'Gender equality is the right thing to do. And it is also smart economics.'

As multiple resources confirm, the most persuasive arguments for men to support diversity are business case arguments that help overcome the zero-sum thinking; it is important to demonstrate how gender diversity is better for everyone, not just women. When it comes to the business case, the proof is in the numbers. On a macro-level, a recent report from McKinsey Global Institute estimated that US\$12 trillion could be added to global growth by advancing gender equality. Even at the individual company level, there is a correlation between financial performance and female leadership. Furthermore, diversity and cultural dexterity help companies reach out to new customer audiences, improve and deepen the talent pool, and foster a greater diversity of ideas and innovation which leads to increased profitability.

Finally, as highlighted by The Catalyst Research, men are often unaware of the personal benefits of gender equality: improved psychological and physical health; more rewarding relationships with women; freedom to share financial responsibilities with a female spouse or partner; freedom to be more involved with children and freedom from limiting masculine gender norms.

Activist Tony Porter sums up these benefits nicely in his *TED Talk: Call to Men* in which he encourages men to challenge the *man box*. 'It's okay to not be dominating, that it's okay to have feelings and emotions, that it's okay to promote equality, that it's okay to have women who are just friends and that's it, that it's okay to be whole, that my liberation as a man is tied to your liberation as a woman. I remember asking a nine-year-old boy, "What would life be like for you, if you didn't have to adhere to this man box?" He said to me, "I would be free".'

CHALLENGES IMPACTING WOMEN

Women face a combination of internal and external challenges that hinder their road to professional success. Men are often naïve about the formidable challenges women face. Although we live in a more progressive and equal global society, women's progress has lagged behind in several critical areas, with Covid-19 only further widening these gaps and magnifying inequalities. What follows are the most common challenges women face that are important for allies to be aware of.

INTERNAL CHALLENGES

While conducting research for *Her Way To The Top*, I surveyed 300 women from around the world. Their responses revealed a great deal about common impediments. Women and multi-ethnic groups who frequently face external bias and discrimination often develop internal barriers, which impact their sense of self-worth. Oftentimes, this leads to changing their behaviour to fit in; an example is code switching or other blockers including Impostor Syndrome; FOMO (fear of missing out); minority stress; perfectionism; acculturative stress; stereotype threat; inability to self-promote and step up; plus, the fear of failure, judgment, and vulnerability. Traditionally, women and other under-represented groups (including ethnic minorities , those with disabilities or people identifying as LGBTQI+) are accustomed to being ignored, trivialised, and debased. In particular, Black, Asian, and Multi-Ethnic women face twice the roadblocks because often race is a more significant impediment than gender, which many people fail to acknowledge. The TrustRadius Women In Tech Report 2021 survey highlights that 62 percent of all women respondents feel confident that they will earn a promotion within the next two years. However, as the report notes, 'any positivity is undercut by the racial divide in this question' and that's because women of colour are reported to feel less confident than white women about their promotion prospects—and that gap has increased three-fold over the past year. 37 percent of women of colour in tech feel that racial bias is a barrier to promotion. These findings clearly evidence the importance of looking at gender equality in the workplace through an intersectional lens. They also show that the challenges of the pandemic have caused unequal impacts along racial lines.

Minority Stress is the chronically high level of stress stigmatised minority groups experience from poor social support, interpersonal prejudice, and discrimination in a social environment. *Acculturative Stress* refers to the feeling of tension and anxiety that accompanies efforts to adapt to the orientation and values of a dominant culture. These conditions can have a negative influence on physical and mental health disparities such as hypertension and depression. Wellness entrepreneur Natasha Stromberg says, 'When we're in an out group, we question why we're out and we doubt ourselves. Social exclusion—no matter how subtle—is devastating to the human psyche.'

Women and people of colour, in fact most under-represented groups, experience a higher incidence of impostor syndrome. They also commonly face 'stereotype threat' in which they feel at risk of confirming negative stereotypes associated with their social group. When marginalised groups believe they have to represent their entire social group, not just themselves, that additional pressure makes them more vulnerable to Impostor Syndrome and they often feel as if they do not belong. The less you are able to relate to people around you, the less confident and competent you tend to feel. This pressure is especially intense in critical and highly stressful situations.

Racial and gender stereotypes magnify low self-esteem, which in turn trigger the need to exceed expectations and hold oneself accountable to exceedingly high standards. Perfectionism is not just a women-specific issue, but also a multicultural one, wherein the need to excel, prove oneself, and be 'perfect' is entrenched in the mindset of minorities struggling to live up to expectations. Unfortunately, perfectionism is often perceived as a shield that will prevent judgment and social ridicule while alleviating the pain of inadequacy and being 'less than.' Perfectionists fear missing out on assignments, and often spend a painstaking amount of time and effort on excruciating details. The desire to be seen, heard, and taken more seriously may also lead to presenteeism. During an economic crisis, presenteeism is influenced by poor employment conditions, fear of unemployment, and employer/ employee relationships—factors that automatically put women and ethnic minorities at a disadvantage.

The Self-Promotion Gap is triggered by a lack of self-esteem and confidence and that in turn discourages under-represented groups from advocating for themselves, expressing their talents, and showcasing their achievements lest they be labelled as 'braggarts' or as 'trying too hard.'

The fear of failure and vulnerability are natural anxieties that prevent under-represented groups from exposing their vulnerability because they are typically considered weaknesses. Members of marginalised groups will therefore do anything they can to avoid the appearance of not being 'strong enough.' Much like women, ethnic minorities often have to work twice as hard to prove themselves with less cushion for failure. The idea of exposing how they really feel or think can seem dangerous and risky.

Additionally, it's important not to overlook the fact that men and women have different leadership styles because they are based on different thought processes. It's about time we acknowledge those differences openly. Women should not be expected to lead by adopting a male leadership model. Rather it is more helpful to think about women as 'equal but different.'

For example, men tend to be more self-oriented, while women tend to be more community-focused. A woman's decision-making process is unique and even more distinctive when combined with the dynamics and subtleties of her personality and style.

Dr Daniel Amen, author of *Unleash the Power of the Female Brain*, has discovered differences in female and male brain functioning. His research reveals that female brains are more active in almost all areas, especially in the prefrontal and limbic cortex. One study suggests that women have 30 percent more neurons firing at any given time than men do. This supports strengths including empathy, intuition, collaboration, and self-control, but it also makes women more vulnerable to anxiety, depression, pain and insomnia.

For too long, women at the pinnacle of their careers have increasingly adopted male qualities to reach the C-level, but it's at the detriment of their own wellbeing. A recent Stanford Business School study shows that women who can combine male and female qualities accomplish more than everyone else. Recognising these gender-specific traits and leveraging them to succeed requires self-awareness—a quality that the most accomplished leaders embody.

And then there is also the issue of how social and cultural conditioning impacts stereotypes. Many of the women I surveyed recognised an issue that is commonly called the 'gender discount.' In *The Confidence Code*, Lindsay Hudson, Chief Executive Officer of BAE Systems, notes, 'When a man walks in the room, they are assumed to be competent until they prove otherwise. For women, it's the other way around.' Success and likeability are positively correlated for men, but successful women are perceived as overly ambitious and/or bossy. Compounding the issue, professional penalties for men and women are quite different, too.

It's safe to assume that there are social realities that augment female self-doubt. Given these socialised differences between genders, women have developed the aforementioned internal challenges that carry a deeper social context and are closely intertwined.

Finally, women enter the workforce far less confident than their male counterparts. A shortage of female confidence is not a myth—it's quantified, researched and documented. In a media interview, Gill Whitty-Collins shares hilarious (but dismal) story to show male versus female confidence in the corporate world, 'A room of men and women was asked, "Is anyone here an expert on breastfeeding?" And the only one to put a hand up was a man, because his wife had done it,' she says. 'The mothers were all thinking, "Well, I'm not a doctor or a midwife," whereas the man had perfect confidence in his expertise.'

A Girl Guiding study found that while 63 percent of seven-to-10-year-old girls feel confident in themselves, only 31 percent of 17-to-21-year-olds feel that way, with a small percentage believing they have an equal chance of succeeding compared to their male colleagues. Another survey conducted by the American Association of University Women revealed that girls emerge from adolescence with a poor self-image, relatively low expectations from life, and much less confidence in themselves and their abilities compared to boys.

In 2011, the UK's Institute of Leadership and Management discovered that half the female respondents reported self-doubt about their job performance and careers, compared with less than a third of male respondents. Co-author of *Women Don't Ask,* Linda Babcock, found in studies of business school students that women initiate salary negotiations four times less than men do.

Confidence in boys largely remains unfazed as they progress into manhood. However, as girls mature, their need to belong intensifies, and they often adjust their ambitions and even attempt to tame their confidence, so others don't form negative opinions about them. As a result, their confidence takes a beating and the otherwise self-confident 13-year-old eventually gives way to a hesitant, unsure 20 to 30-year-old who thinks twice before owning her success.

According to UN Women, young women experience discrimination based on both gender and age. Critical gaps in skills development and mentorship impact the ability of young women to realise their full potential as leaders. Entry-level working women report the lowest levels of confidence, illustrating a strong need for confidence-building at the onset of a woman's career.

EXTERNAL CHALLENGES

Not every challenge is an internal one. External challenges such as systemic bias, workplace harassment, working in male-dominated industries and organisations, and lack of provisions for working mothers were some of the top external challenges for women I surveyed as research for my first book. These barriers were prevalent across the world. Women expressed their frustration with how many industries and organisations still reek of male misogyny and provide unequal advancement opportunities with male bias permeating every level of decision making. The industries with the most pronounced gender inequality also have the lowest female employment. This structure can be alienating for many women and thus it can take a toll on their self-esteem and performance. Moreover, as highlighted earlier, women are regularly subjected to much harsher standards than men.

The world we work in has been predominantly designed by and for men; oftentimes women work within environments that fail to protect them from sexism, bullying and harassment. Sexual harassment is another deep-rooted problem—a true epidemic that is prevalent across the globe as the alarming statistics indicate. The TrustRadius Women In Tech Report 2021 mentioned earlier cites that 72 percent of women in tech have worked at a company where 'bro culture' is pervasive. This is about the same as the previous year when 71 percent of women reported experiencing 'bro culture.' This culture can manifest in a number of ways and range from an uncomfortable work environment to sexual harassment and assault. The research further noted a stark contrast in how men and women perceived that culture very differently.

One of the most common, yet least reported, forms of gender-based violence is psychological violence, which may or may not include sexual harassment but largely involves women being forced to work in an intimidating, hostile, or humiliating environment. These types of micro-aggressions can negatively impact a woman's career advancement.

While macro-aggressions are systemic and potentially obvious, micro-aggressions are everyday slights and invalidations that women and other marginalised groups regularly experience in day-to-day interactions. These often go unacknowledged and may include sexual objectification, seemingly innocuous compliments, snide remarks couched in sexist language and humour, interruptions, invasion of personal space, remarks targeting physical appearance/ race/faith/sexual orientation, and dismissal of ideas.

In addition, women often experience 'benevolent sexism'— when some men believe or act as if women are weak and need their protection. Conversely, hostile sexism is easy to spot—angry, explicitly negative attitudes toward women—while benevolent sexism can appear positive and less damaging.

Women are often tempted to brush this experience off as an overreaction or a misunderstanding of benign intent, but, in reality, such behaviour can be insidiously dangerous, as the perpetrator aims to assault the dignity, competence, and self-worth of the target, often leaving her feeling responsible, sabotaged, undermined and confused.

Unconscious bias and ignorance are cited as the two most common causes of such behaviour. Although these subtle and unintentional 'slips of the tongue' may not seem like a big deal, frequent and demeaning comments chip away at the confidence of victims, preventing them from optimal performance. With constant battering comes emotional turmoil that wears down self-esteem and slowly eats away at a woman's mental health and motivation.

There are several areas where women are at a disadvantage. Take, for example, the gender data gap where women trail men by an alarming amount. This has a direct consequence on many aspects of their lives and I touch upon this later in the book. The gender pay gap is another critical issue. As per the report *The State of the Gender Pay Gap in 2021* by Payscale US, in 2021 women earn 82 cents for every dollar earned by men.

The Equal Pay Act was enacted in UK in 1970, but we have yet to achieve equal pay; women lose out on nearly £140 billion a year when compared to their male counterparts. Gender pay gap reporting became mandatory in the UK from 2018 following which pay gap reports indicated that women are paid less than half of the salaries paid to men working at some of the UK's largest companies.

The gender pay gap is measured by hourly wages, but the gap in overall earnings is actually about twice as big as the gap in hourly earnings, because women are more likely to work part-time. 41 percent of UK women work part-time as compared to 13 percent of men, as author Vicky Pryce highlights in *Women vs. Capitalism.*

Similarly, women experience a pension deficit that later affects their retirement. Perhaps one of the most striking reasons for this wage disparity is that pay gap metrics consider pay but do not factor in unpaid household chores. These behind-the-scenes tasks keep people alive and healthy while enabling society to function, but the work is grossly undervalued, taken for granted and/or entirely unpaid. Melinda Gates has called out this gender disparity in 'unpaid work' like childcare, grocery shopping and household chores.

Gates reveals that women worldwide spend an average of four and a half hours per day on unpaid work—more than double the amount of time men spend. These are 24/7 responsibilities that require an on-call attendant at all times. In developing nations, women spend even more time performing unpaid work, which translates into fewer available hours to pursue education, healthcare, and actual paid work that might help support their families.

Women generally adapt to such lifestyle norms and follow the historic model, either by withdrawing from work and becoming temporary home caregivers, or returning to work after raising families but in less productive, lower paid roles that offer greater flexibility. As a result, their return on educational investment and human capital skills drops in relation to men and of women who work full time. There is also an opportunity cost; they lose more potential every year they spend at home caring for the family, as less experience and fewer skills mean women suffer more comparatively from what economists call 'hysteresis.'

According to the Institute of Fiscal Studies (IFS), when women take time off from work to have children, regardless of how they structure their maternity leave and subsequent professional lives, they will have difficulty recovering their previous wage gap. For mothers in the UK, the IFS finds the gap continues increasing to 33 percent by year 12 after the arrival of the first child. This is as striking as it is revealing.

At the *Her Allies* panel discussion, we also discussed the role of media in perpetuating negative stereotypes. Sexuality discourses on social media are shaping how women experience technology, their perceptions of themselves, and ultimately, their education and career choices and goals.

'Ads often convey the idea that women are inherently better at household chores than men,' says Erica Scharrer, Professor of Communication at the University of Massachusetts, Amherst. Back in 2004, Scharrer studied commercials that were on air during a one-week period on primetime television. Of 477 characters depicted completing chores, 305 were women and 159 were men. Among male characters, 50 percent were portrayed as comically inept. By contrast, more than 90 percent of the female characters were portrayed as competent. A blog on Real Simple entitled

Why Women Can't Let Go noted the aforementioned study and recognised that these types of adverts have pervaded the airwaves for so long that they've penetrated our subconscious. That could be why approximately one in three married women surveyed said they were uncomfortable delegating household chores to their spouse.

IMPACT OF COVID-19

In just a matter of weeks, coronavirus became an all-consuming global pandemic wreaking havoc on the business world and our personal and professional lives. Women found themselves facing an unprecedented double bind—they need to manage their careers and ensure family stability across childcare and household needs.

Earlier recessions have demonstrated that disadvantaged people are less resilient financially and socially; some groups even face intersecting and multiple forms of discrimination. It's critical to understand how detrimental the crisis is for women and how that impact differs between genders. Women remain one of the most marginalised groups in many parts of the world; the global pandemic has hit them hard across health, finances, education, family responsibilities and gender violence. Many equality champions recognise that this catastrophe magnifies existing inequalities. Groups that face multiple disadvantages and have fewer financial and social resources to support them, are most vulnerable in any crisis, and women definitely top this list.

As noted earlier, women compose a significant amount of part-time and informal workers around the world. Such jobs are most vulnerable in times of economic uncertainty. The workers who lose these jobs do not have the skills, nor the technology, to enable them to work from home or to retrain for other employment. Following outbreaks, women face more irreconcilable work breaks than men, and while both genders faced lower wages, women have found it harder to realise their pre-break earnings. Health authorities identify women over 60, single mothers and women of colour as the most vulnerable groups. Their pension deficits work against them, augmenting their economic dependence on men.

There has been much discussion about women bearing the brunt of the pandemic in terms of domestic responsibilities that have robbed their time and energy. A research study by three economists, *Gender Inequality in Research Productivity During the Covid-19 Pandemic*, has found the productivity of female economists, measured by research papers published, has decreased relative to male economists since the pandemic began. Women across the globe are already suffering from intense time poverty, with time being even more elusive for working mothers. And during community lockdown, if human behaviour is predictive, it's the mum who handles much of the family needs and household responsibilities (including home schooling), all of which have disproportionately squeezed them. Mired in obligatory domestic duties without a break has left women fatigued and anxious. In an article in the New York Times by Francesca Donner, which shares how the virus has exposed gender fault lines, Nahla Valji, senior gender advisor at UN states, 'It's one of the starkest consequences that we're seeing from this crisis.'

The TrustRadius report further showed that 57 percent of women in tech feel burned out at work this year, compared to 36 percent of men. It added, 'Sociologist Arlie Russell Hochschild pioneered the term *second shift* to describe the historical housework burden that women carry in addition to their normal work hours. In the past year, exacerbated by the pandemic, that second shift got longer for women around the world. 42 percent of women in tech say they took on most of the household work during the pandemic, compared to only II percent of men.'

Unfortunately, isolation has also led to a frightening escalation in domestic violence, with calls to the UK's national abuse hotline rising by an appalling 65 percent, as reported by The National Domestic Abuse helpline, run by the charity Refuge. In Asian and African countries, thousands of women lack access to resources, hotlines and shelters in the best of times; during the pandemic, these shortages are exacerbated by an increasing number of assaults, and victims have been living in fear of the next terrifying blow. Policy makers have failed to identify this link when implementing quarantine measures.

The pandemic has also forced nearly one billion students out of school—that number includes 743 million girls in 185 countries. UNESCO fears that the rising drop-out rates will disproportionately affect adolescent girls. Girls may also find themselves caring for families while boys continue to study. This will only intensify gender gaps in education and lead to increased risk of sexual exploitation, early and unintended pregnancy, and early and forced child marriage. For most of these children, school closures are temporary, but many girls in developing countries may never return to the classroom, reversing progressive programs that made their education possible in the first place.

In addition, the pandemic has adversely impacted women's healthcare. A recent research study examined whether global health policies during previous outbreaks had considered gender impact; Julia Smith, a health policy researcher at Simon Fraser University shares, 'Across the board, gender issues were ignored.'

The gender roles women have traditionally assumed expose them to the virus more than their male counterparts, as evident from SARS and Ebola outbreaks across Africa. The World Health Organisation (WHO) also noted this in its earlier report, which indicated the influence of these gender roles.

Globally, a majority of health care workers are women—nearly 70 percent according to some estimates—and most occupy nursing roles on the front lines. Other roles include caring for the sick, birth attendants, cleaners, laundry workers, and morticians. In these careers, risk of exposure is higher and protections are not on par with other professions.

Compounding the vast PPE shortages, available protection gear often has a unisex design that doesn't always fit women properly and thus makes it extremely uncomfortable. Many women even lack basic feminine hygiene products like pads and tampons; according to some accounts, female nurses in China had difficulty finding these products.

Pregnant women, in addition to increased occurrences of redundancies, also had less access to antenatal care as healthcare facilities have been inundated with Covid-19 patients. In a normal year, the legal advice line run by Pregnant Then Screwed receives about 3,000 calls from women experiencing pregnancy and maternity discrimination at work. 'Since the start of the pandemic, we've given 32,000 women free legal advice in some form,' says Brearley, who has written a book, *Pregnant Then Screwed: The Truth About the Motherhood Penalty and How to Fix It*. Companies, she believes, are taking advantage of the pandemic to remove pregnant women and mothers. Pregnant women are not just worried about their livelihoods but are also terrified about their safety as they are being asked to work in dangerous situations where they could contract Covid. In May 2020, Pregnant Then

Screwed conducted research with nearly 2,600 pregnant workers and found that a quarter of those working in the NHS were caring for Covid patients. Among BAME women, it was nearly a third.

Furthermore, in many countries, fewer women than men have health insurance, and thus uninsured women have inadequate access to quality care, which produces inferior health outcomes.

The Women and Equalities Committee has been concerned, pointing out how the Government's priorities for recovery are heavily gendered in nature. Investment plans that are skewed towards male-dominated sectors have the potential to create unequal outcomes for men and women, exacerbating existing inequalities. They have also highlighted the need for schemes to support employees and the self-employed to be informed by an Equality Impact Assessment, drawing on evidence of existing inequalities.

Now, more than ever, we must implement interventions in a way that do not perpetuate harmful gender norms, discriminatory practices, and inequalities that will only intensify the devastating impact of the pandemic. We all, including you and I, need to expand the conversation and shift behaviours by transcending gender biases, and systemic inequalities.

SECTION ONE

CHALLENGE YOURSELF

'Everyone thinks of changing the world,
but no one thinks of changing himself.'
-Leo Tolstoy-

Challenging yourself is perhaps the most important phase of your journey. Once you are open to making changes in your everyday interactions, other phases will follow more naturally. It is critical to reflect on your own thoughts and behaviours. Your thoughts are your inner dialogue. Very simply, you want to become aware of what you tell yourself inside so that you—rather than your emotions and biases—direct your choices. To contribute to a more inclusive world, we all have to transform how we behave and challenge old, harmful patterns. Accept that no matter how good you are, chances are there are still many things you are unaware of—knowing what you don't know is the first part of any allyship journey.

As you start this journey, it is important to believe in yourself—convince your brain that it can and will achieve what you want it to do. If you perceive this transformation as a liability, then that is the message you deliver to your brain and your brain produces states that make it a reality. If you change your frame of reference with fresh perspective or mirrored thought, you can change the way you respond in life.

While you are working on self-awareness, mindfully adjust your attitude and imagine a positive outcome. Remind yourself that if you act on change early and modify your expectations accordingly, it will be much easier to adapt.

Your brain will do exactly as it's told. If you keep telling yourself that you can do something, you will be amazed to see how well your brain cooperates in reaching that goal. And that's precisely why repeatedly feeding your brain with positive affirmations is important when challenging yourself or others. Ultimately, you own and control the most powerful weapon that can help you to get out of your own way—your brain. Do not underestimate its power; it will play a pivotal role in making your efforts successful and empower you to make well-informed decisions, free from personal biases and subjectivity. Many of us are victims of our minds. Just as we can get in shape with the right diet and exercise, you are capable of overcoming any prior conditioning of your mind, as long as you are willing to do the work. By repeatedly telling your brain that it can achieve something and following the above techniques, you can train it to think affirmatively. As Henry Ford aptly put it, 'Whether you think you can, or you think you can't, you're probably right.'

Here are many ways you can hold yourself accountable.

EDUCATE YOURSELF

Many men agree they have a critical role to play in D&I efforts, especially initiatives to eliminate gender bias. Yet, too often men are an untapped resource to advance valuable equality programs. The Catalyst Report's findings indicate that individuals must first recognise inequality exists before they will support efforts to address it.

Hence, before you learn about what you need to do, it would be helpful to first educate yourself on the issues impacting women. You cannot change or address what you are not aware of. We have already reviewed many of the challenges women face, so at this stage, you are already one step ahead. The next step is to then proactively become part of the discussion and begin transforming mindset. At this point, it might also be useful to get some clarity on what you actually want to achieve on your allyship journey. You may find value in some of the benefits highlighted earlier. But which benefits specifically appeal to you? Knowing this will increase your ownership.

Creating an outcomes chart can also help you manage this stage. The latter provides a process wherein you can improve the likelihood of achieving your outcome by testing it from different aspects and identifying resources you have or need to reach your results. Some of these factors include, but are not limited to: the context in which the outcome will be achieved; the resources required; the ecology of your outcome; the desirability of your outcome; the purpose of your outcome; and finally, the process of achieving your outcome (how, when, what, why). State your outcome in positive terms and base it on what you want to happen, not what you want to avoid. Some of the questions can look like these:

- What do you want? What is your goal on this journey?
- Why do you want the outcome? What value does it serve?
- What, where, when and with whom will this outcome be achieved?
- What are the internal and external resources required to realise this outcome?
- What indicates that you have achieved the outcome?

- What is the evidence?
- What will you gain or lose by achieving this outcome?
- What is your action plan?
- How will you monitor progress or deal with interference?

Once you have answered these questions, it's time to move on, you can keep revisiting this outcome frame which may evolve over time.

RECOGNISE YOUR PRIVILEGE

Recognising privilege is crucial to understanding how unequal access to power and resources impact communities. Privilege is a set of unearned benefits and advantages assigned to people within a specific social group. Members of a privileged group often do not recognise that they are privileged, whether it is due to their gender, skin colour or another factor. When you belong to a privileged or powerful group, you do not need to draw attention to yourself as a specific entity because you have status. What's more, others perceive you as the standard versus an outlier. But when you belong to an under-represented group, the 'usual' dynamics shift, thus it's important to be wary of those changes. It takes significant self-reflection and scrutiny to begin looking at things differently. To give an example, when we discuss the 'feminisation of poverty' we rarely consider its other side—the 'masculinisation of wealth.'

In describing activist Criado Perez, journalist Nicci Gerrard sums this issue up perfectly: 'Criado Perez has a genius for seeing things that the rest of us miss, and for bringing invisible women out of the shadows, directing our attention to history's forgotten narratives. She has an unerring, unnerving sense of social and cultural blind spots and recognises absence, the space between the lines. We live in a world in which men are the default humans; we don't realise women aren't there because they've always been not-there, and we've never known anything different.'

Being a member of a privileged group does not mean you never struggled; it simply means you haven't faced the same impediments that others may have faced. It's also very important to understand the concept of intersectionality, which Wikipedia describes as 'an analytical framework for understanding how aspects of a person's social and political identities combine to create different modes of discrimination and privilege. Examples of these aspects include gender, caste, sex, race, class, sexuality, religion, disability, physical appearance, and height.' While all humans may experience some degree of disadvantage in their lives, for others, those disadvantages simply multiply given their unique attributes.

Some of the most obvious physical characteristics and circumstances that can differentiate people at work include but may not be limited to: age, likes or preferences; physical ability; mental health; socioeconomic background; sexual orientation; marital status; pregnancy and maternity; accent; and even family responsibilities. Challenges in these areas will impact everyone equally irrespective of gender or race. But if you add ethnicity, race or faith into the equation, those aspects multiply the hindrances. Women of colour, trans women or women with disabilities, often experience amplified marginalisation.

It is also worthwhile to understand the additive identity model versus single-determinant identity models. A single determinant model of identity presumes that one aspect of identity, i.e. gender, dictates one's access to, or disenfranchisement, from power. According to *Demarginalising the Intersection of Race and Sex: A Black Feminist Critique of Antidiscrimination Doctrine, Feminist Theory and Antiracist Politics*, observing the challenges on a single categorical axis is problematic because it often obscures discrete sources of discrimination. For example, in a gender discrimination claim, the racial contours may be overlooked or not given due importance.

However, researcher, educator and writer Mary Maxfield argues that this additive model may set us up for 'Oppression Olympics,' a term coined in the early 1990s, which describes how white supremacy and the patriarchy suppress communities differently. Essentially, the Oppression Olympics triggers the fear of being left behind when the focus shifts to one group's fight for liberation. This fear is unwarranted, as noted earlier, various marginalised groups experience different types of repression and it's important to understand unique issues surrounding each community.

Anti-Black racism and Anti-Asian Hate campaigns are global issues unique to Black and Asian communities around the world, respectively. Supporting these messages doesn't mean you support other issues of injustices and inequalities any less. Mary Maxfield considers this forced ranking of oppression to be unhelpful, lacking empathy and impossible to assess. Moreover, she adds another important angle, the struggle is not just about this and that, but how this and that are so interwoven that you can't actually tell them apart and distinguish clearly where one stops and the other begins. She notes, 'It's about how multiple forms of oppression are experienced simultaneously in ways that make them inextricable from each other. In the middle of the 8th/Pine intersection, you can't say whether you're on 8th or Pine. You're on 8th Pine; it's both, it's more than both, it's mixed.' Crenshaw argued the intersection of oppression means that racism changes the shape of the sexism and the sexism changes the shape of the racism.

Mary Maxfield further reaffirms the need for learning the history of oppression in the US (and in the UK too) not as a single story or a series of separate stories (the racism history, the sexism history, etc), but as a dysfunctional collection of interlocking stories that enable us to challenge the status quo better. Here, she references the terrible Atlantic shootings of eight women, six of whom were Asian American. Many considered this horrific act of violence as misogynistic versus racist, but Mary describes it as an 'age-old version of what misogyny looks like when it targets Asian women. It couldn't be more racist if it tried.'

She adds: 'It's only when we can see the ways that racism and sexism (and all the other-isms) are fusing together in particular ways that we can challenge them effectively. And the point isn't to try and figure out whose version of sexism is most heinous. The point is to try and understand how sexism is operating against different populations of women so we can begin to fight for all women.' And she notes that while Crenshaw spoke specifically of Black women, this can apply broadly across the different axes of identity including ability, sexual orientation, weight, etc. It also applies to other women of colour including AAPI, Native, Latina, Middle Eastern women and others.

As an ally, it's important to understand these concepts, acknowledge your privilege, be mindful of others in less powerful positions and leverage your status to support them in an authentic, meaningful way.

BE TRANSPARENT AND AUTHENTIC

Being an ally means modelling the right behaviour and communicating fairly. And that means stepping out of your comfort zone, entering spaces or conversations that make you uneasy, even if that involves a gaffe or two. To err is to be human; don't be critical of yourself for not knowing the perfect answers—learn as you go. Even the most seasoned allies are continuously learning. Accept your privilege, embrace your inherent bias, but most importantly, be prepared to take action and improve.

During vulnerable times, it's more important for you to demonstrate empathy than caution. Many well-intentioned and sincere men are conflicted about what to do and they are equally afraid to say the wrong things. As a woman, I can honestly admit that most of us would appreciate authenticity above anything else. Don't wait too long to express your concern, even if you're uncertain and still trying to understand the situation.

Reach out to female colleagues, be as transparent as you can, and share what you know while being honest about what you don't know. After all, 'you don't know, what you don't know'—be open to having your awareness raised. And if there's any miscommunication, be quick to rectify and apologise—spare the audacity—people will acknowledge genuine intent more than a half-hearted cover-up. Also, don't assume you know what's best. Check to see if your colleague is comfortable with what is being said while acknowledging your fears; being vulnerable and sharing your imperfections, doubts and mistakes.

Julie Kratz, Founder of Pivot Point, encourages you to share your own diversity story—a time when you felt different, a time when you were the only one in the room, or a time when you felt as if you did not belong. Such stories can engage people and spark meaningful dialogue. However, also keep in mind that not everyone will open up, despite your best intentions. Individuals have different coping mechanisms, so if they don't wish to engage yet, give them space and time.

ASK

Having a woman or woman of colour in your circle is not a

guarantee that you are an antiracist or feminist ally. The only way to become an ally 'in the know' is to ask the right questions. The more you know, the easier it will be to help colleagues feel more comfortable. It can be difficult to ask questions, however, it's far better to ask than to be ignorant. I recently attended a D&I panel discussion in which one of the panellists, Laurie Morgen, summed this perspective up as follows, 'You are so scared of being offensive that you are being offensive.' I have attended many events in the past few years, but only a small number of attendee questionnaires asked me in advance if I had any overlooked needs or dietary requirements. I am thrilled when I am asked this question because I feel included, respected and considered.

As pointed out earlier, it is impossible to anticipate everyone's needs and expectations, but by asking respectful questions, you are better equipped to provide support. That said, how you ask is as important as what you ask. You do not want to sound intrusive, just naturally curious and genuinely interested in finding out answers. Your questions should seamlessly fit into casual conversations without crossing personal boundaries. Thoughtful questions can often clarify what others have already said. That entails paraphrasing, 'Are you saying. . .?' or prompting, 'Do you mean. . .?' or 'So, if I understand you correctly. . .'.

Here are some open-ended questions that seek to respectfully gather information:

- What's one thing I can do as an ally to remove obstacles to your advancement?
- What do you think we can do about this?
- What would you like me to stop doing?
- Would it be helpful if I. . .?
- Supposing we were to. . .?

49

- Can you please help me understand where you're coming from?
- Can we set a time to talk about the changes we're both prepared to make?
- I'm prepared to. . . Would that help the situation?
- Probing is a helpful form of open questioning that can lead you to a deeper level of understanding within your conversations. One of the most common ways of probing is to ask an open question, such as:
- Can you describe that in more detail for me?
- Can you give me a specific example of what you mean?
- What do you think we should do?

The difficulty here is that if you ask too many probing questions, the other person may see it as an invasion of privacy. The summary question is another method that can be effective as a conversation in winding down. For example, 'You have tried ignoring your colleague's aftershave and shared with him how it affects your allergies. You have tried shutting your door to keep the scent out of your workspace. None of these solutions has worked and now you are asking me to intervene. Is that correct?'

I am a huge fan of surveys and polls that can help build awareness while capturing experiences and perspectives. It is important to hear directly from people you want to form an alliance with so you understand their challenges and needs. Another way to do this is to create opportunities for women by establishing networks to share grievances.

In a recent survey we conducted via The Grey Area, nearly 50 percent of people revealed they lack avenues to communicate challenges at work. In her book, *The Incredible Power of Staff Networks*, Cherron Inko-Tariah MBE cautions us against superficial efforts to establish and join networks if you aren't committed to their objectives.

Also, bear in mind that some women may already be sensitive about over-sharing personal information or grievances, as it exposes their vulnerability and they fear being blamed. In addition, under-represented communities have a long-standing history of repeated discrimination and not being listened to, which may make them sceptical. Thus, inauthentic actions and any appearance of superciliousness or presumption may be triggering and could backfire.

LISTEN

Establishing common ground, trust and rapport in business relationships begins with effective listening. Listening is more of an attitude, a desire to understand what others are communicating. Many of us do not listen very well; we pretend we are listening when we really aren't and that can create more of an issue with the person sharing. Active listening involves making a conscious effort to hear and understand the message, while being conscious of the non-verbal aspects of the conversation.

- What are the speaker's facial expressions, hand gestures and posture telling us?
- Is her voice loud or shaky?
- Is she stressing certain points?
- Is she mumbling or having difficulty finding the words?

When you are listening to someone, these techniques or demonstration cues show a speaker that you are paying attention, providing you are not acting them out. Responding to the speaker's feelings also adds an extra dimension to listening, validates their message and builds rapport.

Physical indicators include making eye contact, nodding your head from time to time, and leaning in to the conversation. You can also give verbal cues or use phrases such as, 'Uh-huh,' 'Go on,' 'Really!' and 'Then what?'

Rapport means showing an individual that you understand, support and respect them as human beings. This doesn't mean that you have to agree with everything they say, but rather focusing on understanding their perspective. Once you have established a basic connection, perhaps by identifying something in common and establishing a mutual sense of trust, then you can work on developing and deepening the relationship.

Here are some other strategies recommended by Velsoft Training Academy that can improve how much you retain and help build relationships, so that others know you are actively engaged and receptive to their message.

- **Make a decision to listen:** Close your mind to clutter and noise and look at the person speaking to you. Give them your undivided attention.
- **Don't interrupt others**: Make it a habit to let them finish what they are saying. Respect that they have thoughts they are processing and sharing, and wait to ask questions or comment when they have finished.
- **Keep your eyes focused on the speaker and your ears tuned to his/her voice:** Don't let your eyes wander around the room, just in case your attention does too. At the same time, also bear in mind that cultural norms surrounding eye contact may influence how the speaker chooses to maintains eye contact and communicate.

- **Carry a notebook or start a conversation file on your computer**: Write down all the discussions that you have in a day. Capture the subject, who spoke more (where you listening or doing a lot of the talking?), what you learned in the discussion, as well as the who, what, when, where, why and how aspects of it. Once you have conducted this exercise eight to 10 times, you will be able to evaluate what level your listening skills are at.

Let's take a look at the problems that can obstruct passive listening when speaking to a female colleague and some possible solutions to overcome them.

You decided in advance that she—or what she will say—will be uninteresting
This may lead you to tune out. Instead, tell yourself you will make a real effort to learn something new during the conversation and put effort into listening.

You were distracted when listening
Choose an area without distractions. Refuse to be distracted.

You did not adjust to what she was saying. For example, you were talking about the weather but the topic has now shifted to what she did on vacation
This requires mental agility. You could ask her to slow down and give you time to shift gears.

You took too many notes
Rather than copy down every word, just note key points. This takes practice but is worth mastering.

You believed that what was being said was too difficult to understand so you tuned out
Ask questions to clarify or request that she illustrate the point.

You got side-tracked by your own biases
Let's say she used the word 'refugee' to refer to the people left homeless by a flood or earthquake. You prefer the word 'victim.' This may be important to you but try not to raise this point until she has had the opportunity to complete her thoughts.

You jumped in too soon to relate your own ideas or experiences
Be patient. Listen. Give the other person a turn to speak, then present your ideas or experiences, if appropriate. More tips on 'mansplaining' later on.

You were daydreaming
Self-discipline is required to listen. Bring yourself back to the conversation by internally saying 'stop.' Remember to make eye contact to connect with her. This will also help you stay engaged.

Have you ever been guilty of any of these? How could you avoid this behaviour in the future?

PREPARE TO BE UNCOMFORTABLE

When you ask questions with the intention to improve, chances are there will be unexpected feedback involved, which could be awkward, even unpleasant. Do your own work in advance, especially before engaging in difficult conversations. Self-awareness, but more importantly, self-control, are important to develop gender empathy.

As human beings, we are wired to react when attacked, but don't give in to that urge. The authors of *Crucial Conversations* point out that when we are faced with pressure and strong opinions, we stop worrying about the goal of adding to the pool of meaning and start looking for ways to win, punish or keep peace. However, don't dismiss, create positive spin, get defensive or make excuses.

When opinions vary, emotions can run high, but it is the perfect time to refocus your brain and find your bearings. *Crucial Conversations* recommends this, 'First clarify what you want and then clarify what you don't want. Ask yourself what you want for yourself, the other person and the relationship. Search for the 'and'.' For example: 'I want to help my colleague deal with a challenge and not appear self-righteous or demanding.' Approaching any conversation with this kind of open mind will lessen the sting.

ACKNOWLEDGE YOUR RESPONSIBILITY

Everyone occasionally commits a faux pas in the workplace, but what matters most is admitting your mistake and learning from it. Gender savviness and aptitude are informed by experience. The best allies are not afraid to make mistakes because their intentions are genuine.

An apathetic person is dismissive and will not typically engage, so if someone offers you feedback, it's because they care.

Here are some thought starters on how to respond to constructive criticism:

- I appreciate the trust you have shown by giving me this candid feedback.
- Thank you for bringing this to my attention.

- I sometimes get excited and tend to interrupt but that isn't an excuse - I will be more respectful next time.
- I apologise for this slip-up, I am going to do better.
- I recognise that I need to learn/do more.
- I am going to take time to reflect on this.
- I appreciate the effort you have put in.
- How can I make this better/right?
- I am glad you asked that question. Let's talk about it.
- I believe you/I hear you.
- I appreciate that I should have said something earlier.

If you are open to being challenged, also be willing to apologise.

ACKNOWLEDGE YOUR BIAS

Yes, you are biased—we all are!

As human beings, we have a natural tendency to judge and form internal biases, but we can unlearn harmful tendencies and behaviours. Using a Neuro Linguistic Programming (NLP) lens, you appreciate that each individual has their own unique map of the world shaped by lived experiences. Moreover, to process information, our brain creates filters and shortcuts. Without these shortcuts, we would have to sift through an overload of information—even routine and mundane tasks. But brain shortcuts have a downside; they can compartmentalise patterns based on the cumulative effect of everything we have been exposed to in our entire life, thereby oversimplifying or even generalising things. Moreover, all this is happening in the back of our minds, which means we may not be aware that we are acting/reacting in a certain way.

Take, for example, affinity bias. People like to work with others they feel comfortable with. A man generally feels more comfortable working with another man, but if many team members share the same life experiences, they will miss out on all other perspectives. Often, we refuse to acknowledge this or any other type of bias. Too often we hear people say that we don't see colour or gender. But as Vernā Myers, VP, Inclusion Strategy at Netflix, points out in her TED Talk, *'The problem was never that we saw colour. It was what we did when we saw colour.'* Vernā calls it the false ideal because while we're busy pretending not to see, we are not being aware of the ways in which racial or gender differences are changing people's possibilities and preventing them from thriving.

Therefore, it's crucial to identify your triggers and keep them in check. Ask yourself if there are any precipitating factors clouding your judgment. If you are already frustrated, or have had a bad experience with a certain person or the group they represent, that triggered response can make you angry that much faster. Are you walking along any historical emotional tracks and unable to view a situation dispassionately?

Question the following negative limiting beliefs:

- **Emotional reasoning:** Assuming your negative emotions (and those of the majority) are proof of the way things really are.
- **Personalisation/blame:** Holding someone personally responsible for an event that is not entirely under their control.
- **Mental filter:** Picking out a single negative detail and dwelling on it.
- **Magnification:** Exaggerating a personal flaw, small negative experience, or someone else's abilities.
- **Labelling:** Resorting to simplistic and negative labels to

define behaviour. Sometimes, differences in preferences lead to women being unintentionally excluded. A man's behaviour often changes when he is amongst other men, and their sports-talk may not sound inclusive. No matter how well intentioned you are, consider that you may be unaware of the nuances of a female perspective, thus you may risk coming across as ignorant or condescending.

When evaluating your own biases, ask yourself the following questions:

- Is this belief/assumption always true?
- Am I making any assumptions on the basis of gender, race, sexual orientation, faith, age, or ability?
- Is my belief based on limited and incomplete knowledge?
- What proof/evidence is there to support my belief or negate it?
- What other factors do I need to consider?
- What would someone I trust think of my conclusion?
- Who says things should be this way?
- How else might I view this situation?
- Am I not accepting responsibility for something which is my fault or within my control?
- What am I not seeing or acknowledging?
- What could be a more enabling belief?
- What could be the impact of what I say or do?
- What is the opportunity cost of inaction?

Questioning yourself in this manner can distance you from debilitating biases and enable you to view situations objectively. You can subvert each bias by testing its validity through a belief-audit that allows you to identify holes in your thinking. You can't control what people around you will think and say, but you can control your own reaction and avoid negativity.

DON'T MAKE ASSUMPTIONS

Men may sometimes assume they are better informed and more capable than their 'fragile' female colleagues; as Gill Whitty-Collins describes it, 'They may even believe they can make female-oriented decisions based on something their wife once said.' However, as an ally you will avoid making assumptions about habits, preferences, choices and aptitude based solely on gender. Kristen Pressner recommends, 'Flip it to test it, which is essentially flipping your comment/question to see if you would still say it or ask it if you weren't addressing a woman.' Questions surrounding career choices are far too common for women, and they often receive pushback from others who think they are stepping outside of gender norms. It is common to assume a person's profession based on age, gender or race. It is also common to assume gender based on a particular profession (i.e. a nurse is assumed to be a woman). Dr Suzanne Wertheim calls these inferences *unconscious demotions.*

One of the survey respondents for my book *Her Way To The Top* shared how her new boss did not invite her to dinners. Instead of sulking, Alicia chose to confront the issue by carefully working this into a conversation with her boss. She believed creating awareness of an issue and respectfully communicating concerns in a subtle way are the first steps toward changing behaviours. If you are a man reading this, then know this strategy can be equally valuable for you.

Alicia also recalled the time when she wasn't offered a role because her boss wrongly assumed the more demanding nature of the role might not suit her as 'a woman.' Alicia later addressed this issue when she answered a diversity study question about what it was really like to be a woman. She explained to her boss how important it is for colleagues to treat women working in the office as team members and professionals first, and as women second. She made her boss realise that women contend with incorrect assumptions and inappropriate questions on a regular basis. That valuable exchange was eye-opening for her boss. Effective communication can change future behaviour in positive ways. When her boss had an open position and a qualified pregnant employee, he asked her if she wanted the role instead of assuming that she wouldn't.

This is the perfect segue into an issue known as 'mansplaining,' a practice in which men sometimes offer unwarranted advice and assume the role of expert in an attempt to share their superior knowledge. This unsolicited advice is often poorly received, especially when the women listening are more knowledgeable than the male speaker assumed. To avoid this issue, ask yourself the following questions before jumping in to intervene:

- Do they need an explanation or have they explicitly asked for it?
- Am I making assumptions about my own superior knowledge or competence?
- Is sharing the opinion relevant to the conversation?
- Is gender/race or any other bias impacting my interpretation of the above?

Your answers to these questions are critical. Improved self-awareness helps you coach yourself toward objective, balanced decision-making and behaviours.

AVOID STEREOTYPING AND GENERALISING

The racially diverse groups you work with might not fit the stereotypes society defines for that group, so avoid clustering communities and their respective issues. It's helpful to understand that although a majority of women and marginalised groups have likely experienced prejudice at some point, certain challenges may only be unique to specific ethnicities. Even women from the same social groups might not fit the stereotypes that society defines for their group. A Black colleague's experience may be different from that of an Asian colleague; hence it's important not to generalise, cluster, digress, or dilute the barriers respective communities face. Moreover, some people experience multiple disadvantages due to gender, faith, race, ability, socioeconomic background, and/ or sexual orientation. Take, for example, a Black Muslim woman who may experience prejudice based on her skin colour, gender, and faith.

Aspire to understand unique experiences and identities; your advice or questions may not be suited for women of colour or other marginalised groups so do not offer one-size-fits-all solutions. For example, most Muslim women are often victims of an assumptive, stereotypical but widely prevalent depiction which sees them as subservient, subjugated or in need of rescuing. As a practicing Muslim woman of colour who is proud of her identity, I personally find this naive generalisation offensive.

Recently, a Muslim woman achieved a historic milestone that most were keen to acknowledge and celebrate. However, one particular media interview was excruciatingly disappointing as she was not only talked over but cornered and click-bated through irrelevant questioning in a manner which was both divisive and disparaging. The interviewer seemed to be showboating, lacking awareness, research or insights, and was almost desperate to extract an answer that could feed into a pigeon-holed narrative of the interviewee's faith.

Marginalised groups already experience what is known as stereotype threat. Unfortunately, most micro aggressions committed against marginalised groups are said to be done unconsciously, unintentionally or under the guise of 'genuine intrigue'. Those at the receiving end tend to 'cover' facets of their identity to avoid judgement and labelling, which in turn prevents them from showing up authentically.

To truly promote belongingness, we need to stop making these people uncomfortable and awkward and avoid signalling out/ challenging or generalising any aspects of their values or belief system, otherwise we will only risk fuelling harmful stereotypes, which can torpedo self-esteem and performance.

Now, let's have a look at gender blind spots (GBS); beliefs, habits and stereotypes we learn in childhood about how to behave based on gender, and how they have a significant impact on women's careers. These also present major obstacles to businesses when working to improve diversity and inclusion.

In my first book, I shared research on how girls and boys socialise differently. Society rewards girls for being good, not audacious, for being cooperative and compliant, but not impudent. So, there's little surprise that is exactly what they do: 'put their heads down and play by the rules.'

Gender rules become unconscious in adulthood and continue to profoundly impact our habits, assumptions and beliefs about how to work, interact and socialise. And even though as some scholars assert, innate gender differences do not exist in certain areas, most of us mature as adults with stereotypes fully entrenched in our psyches.

Her Way To The Top highlights how there is a stereotypical expectation from women to be 'nice,' communal and nurturing. And when they defy these expectations and reach out for opportunities, just like men do, it creates dissonance in peoples' minds and these women are judged ill-favourably. More success leads to more vitriol, not just from men, but females too. Many women who have reached the pinnacle have reported unrelenting waves of prejudice. 'Damned if you do and damned if you don't.'

Another common misconception relates to introversion—introverted female leaders are often treated differently and experience unfavourable bias. My very good friend and author of *Quietly Invisible*, Carol Stewart, notes, 'For many, it's putting on a mask and suppressing their authentic voice as they try to put on a persona that makes them feel accepted. . .'

On two different occasions, I have interviewed a male and female candidate who both appeared introverted. When we regrouped to assess the merits of each candidate, the hiring team judged the introverted woman far less favourably than the introverted man. The man was described as cool and collected and his answers evaluated as insightful and calculated, while the introverted woman, despite similar behaviours, was labelled shy, unsure and too reserved.

Here are some additional ways we discriminate by gender.

Forms of Address
We should be consistent in how we refer to all genders. It's common for men to be addressed as professors or doctors, however, women with the same professional title are often addressed by first name only. A BBC Breakfast presenter issued a public apology when it was flagged how the man being interviewed was addressed as a professor but his female colleague wasn't.

As per advice from The National Centre for Transgender Equality, it's important not to make assumptions about people's gender because you can't tell if someone is non-binary simply by looking at them, just like you can't tell if someone is transgender just by how they look. The website further recommends, 'If you're not sure what pronouns someone uses, ask. Non-binary people may use different pronouns. Many non-binary people use *they* while others use *he* or *she*, and still others use other pronouns. Asking whether someone should be referred to as *he*, *she*, *they*, or another pronoun may feel awkward at first, but is one of the simplest and most important ways to show respect for someone's identity.'

UN Women suggests that when preference is unknown for addressing women, precedence is given to Ms over Mrs, as the former is more inclusive and can refer to any woman, regardless of marital status. UN Women also suggests avoiding gender-biased expressions or expressions that reinforce gender stereotypes.

Such examples of discriminatory, gendered, or bias questions and statements include the following as well as those in the table on the next page:

- I am not sexist/racist but. . .
- You are so young!
- Is that your real hair?
- You are in the wrong room.
- Where are you actually from?
- Your English is so good. You are articulate.
- Where were you born?

Women/Girls	Men/Boys
She throws/runs/fights like a girl.	Do it in a manly way.
She makes the office more beautiful/pleasant/nice.	Don't be a sissy.
Women are supposed to be nurturing.	Men don't cry like girls.
You should smile more.	Don't cry/walk/talk like a girl.
Is it that time of the month?	Men need to be rock solid/providers/tough.
When are you having kids?	Men just don't understand.
Who is taking care of your kids?	You need to man-up/don't be weak.
She is too caring/nice/compassionate to be a leader.	You are meant to provide and protect.
Don't play the race/gender card!	The value of a man is determined by his wealth/car/house/bank balance.
She is not a cultural fit.	That's women's work.
I'd like to see her prove her mettle.	
She is too aggressive/emotional/weak/indecisive/crazy/hysterical.	
She is a nag/too moody.	
We don't want to lower the bar.	
Do you wear a hijab out of choice?	
Hey hon/girl/sweetheart/kiddo/darling/child.	
As a girl/woman you don't need to study/earn that much.	
Guys/girls.	

To avoid discriminatory language, reverse the gender and check whether the meaning or emphasis of the sentence changes or sounds odd. Examples:

- Don't cry like a boy.
- Men do not need to study/earn as much.

Discrimination is also evident when using either/or feminine and masculine pronouns. Gender-inclusive English communication uses the masculine form by default, which can be avoided. For example, 'every permanent representative must submit his credentials to protocol.'

If it's not relevant to the communication, it is best to avoid using any gender specific pronouns at all.

Other examples of inclusive language from UN Women:

Strategy	Less Inclusive	More Inclusive
Using plural pronouns/adjective	A staff member in Antarctica earns less than **he** would in New York	A staff member in Antarctica earns less than **one** in New York.
Use the pronoun one	If a complainant is not satisfied with the board's decision, **he** can ask for a rehearing	A complainant **who** is not satisfied with the boards's decision can ask for a rehearing

Strategy	Less Inclusive	More Inclusive
Use the relative pronoun *who*	A substitute judge must certify that he has familiarised himself with the record of the proceedings.	Substitute judges must certify that they have familiarised themselves with the record of the proceedings.
Use a plural antecedent	A person must reside continuously in the territory for 20 years before he may apply for permanent residence.	A person must reside continuously in the territory for 20 years before applying for permanent residence.
Omit the gendered word	The author of a communication must have direct and reliable evidence of the situation he is describing	The author of a communication must have direct and reliable evidence of the situation being described
Gender neutral words	mankind manpower manmade firemen	humankind/human race/humanity staffing artificial/ human-caused firefighter

Catalyst recognises that gender bias is so ingrained in society, it's almost automatic and how even the most progressive among us can be guilty of it. To address this bias, they launched a powerful #biascorrect plug-in, an equality tool that helps users spot their own unconscious bias in everyday conversations and empowers them to actively work against it. I would highly recommend visiting their website https://www.catalyst.org/biascorrect/.

AVOID UNDERMINING WOMEN THROUGH THESE HARMFUL PRACTICES

- **Manterrupting:** When a man unnecessarily interrupts a woman.
- **Bropropriating:** When a man takes credit for a woman's idea.
- **Hepeating:** When a woman suggests an idea, it's ignored, but then a guy says the same thing and everyone loves it.
- **Mansplaining:** When a man explains something to a woman in a patronising way. It often begins with a man disregarding a woman's opinions by interrupting her mid-sentence.
- **Manels:** Panels composed of only men.
- **Gas lighting:** When an individual uses psychological manipulations that sow seeds of doubt in members of targeted groups, making them question their own memory, perception and sanity.
- **Off-topic questions or showboating:** When individuals ask irrelevant questions to challenge the credibility of a presenter (often a member of a marginalised group) and to showcase their own intelligence. This is a power play to distract someone in a position of authority.

- **Manspreading:** When men sit with their legs spread wide into a V-shaped slouch, effectively occupying two, sometimes even three, seats in a crowded public area.
- **Manslamming:** When a man refuses to alter his pavement trajectory in a crowded place and a collision results.

I feel awkward listing these gendered neologisms given my direction that you should avoid this type of language. Admittedly, these expressions do reek of gender essentialism; the idea that specific physical, social and cultural traits are native to a particular gender. One of the problems with simplistic terms like these is that men will be cautious of what they say and do, just as women are. I am also well aware that you may not be engaging in these behaviours and could very well be a victim of these issues yourself. My purpose here is not to levy accusations and generalise an entire social group. I am against using gender conforming labels, particularly negative ones. However, by and large, these tactics are gendered, and whether men use them consciously or unconsciously, they do make women and diverse racial groups uncomfortable and sabotage their confidence. Awareness of these issues means you will be in a better position to call the behaviour out when you spot it especially where a woman may feel she is not able to.

ENGAGE WITH OTHERS OUTSIDE YOUR CIRCLE

Find ways to prevent female colleagues from feeling isolated. Identify common bonds you share. When there are fewer women in a meeting or boardroom, they are often considered outsiders. To overcome this barrier, it is critical to bridge the gap and identify shared interests. Get to know them as people. Ask them about their families and hobbies. We are all human beings and have similar goals. We have our own fears, dreams and experiences. In this age of radical transparency, open communication helps remove these barriers and foster authentic relationships. In her *TED Talk: How to Overcome Our Biases, Walk Boldly Towards Them*, Vernā *Myers* notes that our biases are the stories we make up about people before we know who they actually are. But how will we know who they are if we are afraid of them and avoid them? So she encourages us to walk towards our discomfort, take inventory, and expand our social and professional circles. Especially, reach out to people missing from your circle and make an effort to know them personally.

Sometimes micro-aggressions occur simply because we are unaware of them. As an ally, the last thing you want to do is deliver unintended slights or micro-aggressions, because you are uninformed about what inappropriate communication sounds like. The more people you meet that are different from you, the more conversant you will be with different cultures and backgrounds thereby ensuring a better chance of overcoming bias, especially affinity bias.

BELIEVE HER

As a supportive male ally, you allow women to educate you on issues they face in the workplace. When they do share a grievance or vent out, believe what they say, without attaching your own assumptions. *Good Guys* warns us to steer clear of the *sexist rescue manoeuvre*. When someone calls out verbal harassment, do not minimise it by saying, 'I am sure he didn't mean it!' Women's complaints are often dismissed or not taken seriously. The Everyday Sexism Project founded by Laura Bates catalogues incidents of everyday sexism, interactions considered 'serious or minor, outrageously offensive or so niggling and normalised that you can't even protest.' The project's site describes how most women get used to the thinking that it is 'just the way things are' so they rarely complain. Those who do object are labelled killjoys, uptight, prudent, militant feminists or accused of overreacting. These monikers can unwittingly squash their perspective. Defending perpetrators and assuming positive intent, centres your feelings on the majority and not the victimised minority. If women are targeted, it is important to acknowledge that it is not their fault, and the harassment has nothing to do with their actions or who they are as a person. Support them by listening and then encouraging them to detach from the emotional charge caused by the abuse. They did not incur this on themselves, nor do they deserve it.

Even if you are cautious of validating before investigating, it is important to practice empathy. To take a more balanced approach and avoid reinforcing a concern, you need not use phrases like, 'I agree' or, 'Yes, that's true.' Simply express your empathy by rephrasing the person's statement.

Appropriate phrases include:

- I hear. . .
- I understand. . .
- Correct me if I'm wrong; what I think you're saying. . .

Rephrasing before answering offers you:

- A chance to empathise with her concerns.
- An opportunity to show the person that you understand the concern.
- A moment to think of an appropriate response.

Often, we do not intend to offend, but intention is not a justification for inappropriate behaviour, especially if it is a repeated offence. Assuming positive intent and invalidating improper behaviour can impact a woman's psychological safety. It is important to be aware that harassment is more about the impact on the recipient and has little to do with intent on the part of the 'aggressor.'

Micro-aggressions can erode a woman's confidence and cause her to check out, little by little. Do not challenge the validity of her encounters, the authenticity of her observations and the truthfulness of her perceptions. Believe her by normalising her experience instead of policing her reaction. If you have witnessed any type of harassment, share your observations with a team leader or Human Resource professional. In fact, *Good Guys* recommends not just validating but becoming a courageous watchdog.

BE VIGILANT

As an ally, it is essential to keep an ear to the ground. To use an analogy suggested by Bill Proudman, CEO of White Men as Full Diversity Partners, in the report Men as Allies, 'Men are like fish in a fishbowl. Because they never have to leave, they never see the water that surrounds them. They must make a conscious effort to see the culture around them—the water in the fishbowl.'

Actively scan your environment to spot visibly unhappy or disengaged female colleagues. *Good Guys* calls it 'sharpening situational awareness and cultural acumen.' While a low grievance and absence rate can indicate a healthy workforce, in actuality, it might reveal a bigger problem. It's important to look deeper for signs of distress; employees can be physically present but mentally absent. Colleagues who seem distracted, depressed, or participate and engage less than usual, may be struggling. If they are solemn, irritable or moody, or otherwise exhibit changes in work patterns or behaviour, they might be facing challenges at work. Conversely, some employees may show no signs at all. Women are quite good at hiding their pain. If you care enough to notice something is amiss, then also be prepared to take action, or at least ask about it. Also, keep an eye on situations that could potentially develop into harassment.

Networks provide opportunities for colleagues to be vulnerable and share their challenges in a safe space. It is helpful to engage with team members via these networks. Attending meetings demonstrates support and can help educate you about the challenges faced by women. You can review your industry's community, online networks and social channels, and participate in company-sponsored affinity and networking groups. Joining different women's business groups and meet-ups allows you to provide ongoing support, understanding and opportunities. You will make new friends and hear diverse perspectives that can sharpen your situational awareness.

SHARE THE WORKLOAD AT HOME

Some say it is the long, hard hours of thankless, unnoticed grunt work that create the foundation of intimacy. Nurturing involves unheralded tasks, like holding someone when they are sick, doing the laundry, ironing, and washing dishes. If you profess to be an ally at work but don't share the same enthusiasm at home, then you have what *Good Guys* calls 'ally dissonance.' This occurs when there is conflict between what you say and what you actually do, especially in private when no one is watching.

Unfortunately, family-friendly workplace reforms are often regarded as women's issues. More accurately, these are parents' issues. The US Census Bureau considers a mother to be the designated parent, even if both parents are present in the home. When a mother is caring for her children, it is called 'parenting,' but when a father takes care of children it is called 'child arrangement.' UK public policy also reinforces that the mother is a child's primary caregiver. Child benefits are paid to mothers while the term 'babysitting' is still widely used for men when they assume childcare responsibilities. It is also seen how men who take leave for the birth of a child or to care for a sick parent are perceived as less committed.

As author Josh Levs explores in his book *All In* (cited in *Scientific American* in an essay by Daniel Barron), men have been fired, demoted or lost job opportunities for taking paternity leave or seeking a flexible schedule, because of stigmas against men as caregivers. So, even when paid paternity leave is available, men often feel they can't take it. Joeli Brearley is the author of *Pregnant Then Screwed: The Truth About the Motherhood Penalty*. In an interview with The Guardian, she shared how she knows of one father on paternity leave who would receive emails from his boss that started, 'Hello, nanny.'

Women across the world are suffering from time poverty. In a survey I conducted for my first book, a large majority of women, irrespective of where they lived, confessed that managing time was the primary challenge holding them back in their careers. The time has now come for men to step in, publicly claim fatherhood and share their pursuit of the elusive work/life balance.

As an ally, you can lighten your partner's workload by sharing household chores. If you are a parent, and especially if you are a senior leader actively participating in your children's lives; doctor appointments, parent teacher meetings, homework, exam prep and engagement proactively demonstrates that these tasks are not just a mother's responsibility alone. Do not shy away from taking parenting leave to support your partner and divide responsibilities that women traditionally fulfil. In many households, Covid-19 has led to a newfound domestic partnership at home, which can be maintained even after normalcy resumes. Of course, leaning in to support your partner does not mean adjourning your own career, but it does mean being an active ally for your partner at home.

WHAT YOU TELL YOUR CHILDREN IS IMPORTANT

Generation Z and Generation Alpha will be tomorrow's leaders. They will lead businesses, communities and perhaps even lead the country one day. By mentoring and inspiring them, we are laying the ground work for a future generation of women and men who have the power to make a difference.

Teach your girls to be kind, not nice. Niceness will not keep them safe. Kindness can, and should, be taught. Niceness, however, springs from a desire to please others, even if it is at our own expense. 'For the most part, "nice" means be tolerant and accommodating,' writes Shefali Tsabary, a clinical psychologist and author of *The Awakened Family*. 'If we are brutally honest with ourselves, it also implies: do whatever it takes to keep the peace.' Instead of teaching our girls to be nice, argues Tsabary, we should teach them how to be themselves, to be self-aware, 'which means self-directed, self-governed, true to themselves.'

In an article about male role models, TV presenter and author June Sarpong shares that while not every man is in an influential position to drive big systemic changes like appointing female Cabinets, men like her father (and mine) can encourage the confidence, academic or creative talents of their daughters and can be their greatest allies. Male colleagues can also encourage the same for women in the workplace, as mentors and advocates. Furthermore, how you treat your partner is going to set the expectation for your own children.

Ziauddin Yousafazi, proud feminist father of Malala Yousafazi, and supporter of my first book, shares his experience challenging gender discrimination in a society which is deeply rooted in patriarchy and male chauvinism. In this book *Let Her Fly*, he writes, 'When I say of Malala "I did not clip her wings," what I mean is that when she was small, I broke the scissors used by the society to clip girls' wings. I did not let those scissors near Malala. I wanted to let her fly high in the sky, not scratch around in a dusty courtyard, grounded by social norms.'

Redempter Batete, a gender specialist with UNICEF, notes that educating boys about women's rights is the logical next step, because if we don't target youth when they are young, then we risk missing out on opportunities to do so as they grow up. Moreover, boys are more receptive to this type of message when they are younger, before they are exposed to gender norms/biases in broader society as they mature.

Similarly, Minister of Gender and Family Promotion, Solina Nyirahabimana, agrees that after 25 years of breaking gender stereotypes by telling women what they can do, 'men have been left behind' in the conversation. And perhaps this is the reason the United Nations launched #HeForShe in September 2014 as a movement to inspire and encourage men to take action against gender inequality. Rallying support from male allies is crucial in our fight for generation equality. It is most effective to start these efforts early. Solina works to prevent discrimination by instilling gender equality principles in children. Girls and boys are encouraged to participate in plays based on what they have learned to combat gender stereotypes. In one scenario, a boy questions his mother's decision to prioritise his education over his sister's, noting he can help with the housework and the task shouldn't be his sister's alone.

Two years ago, when I was explaining the concepts of gender equality and the gender pay gap to my now 10-year-old son Ibrahim, he pointed out that his favourite book series had fewer books for girls than it had for boys, 'Mama, now I know what you mean when you say girls have been getting less. They should make more girl books!' I had never realised that before! I was amazed that he noticed a detail I had missed.

It's equally crucial to dispel the myths of toxic masculinity when mentoring young boys. Ben Hurst from *The Good Lad Initiative* recommends moving to a discussion around positive masculinity, that being, 'a new version of masculinity, one where we celebrate being a man and celebrate all of the good parts of being a man, but also one where we give men spaces to unpack all of the problematic messages that they have learned about what it means to be a man and we give them space to relearn what it means to be a man.'

We already face a long list of challenges due to skewed social conditioning. It is not too late to influence the existing generation and help them think differently. Let's change the dynamics by teaching boys and girls to be responsible, empowered, empathetic individuals who are ready to call out gendered actions or assumptions, hold each other accountable, and positively influence each other's behaviours and beliefs.

SHARE OFFICE HOUSEWORK

Women often take meeting notes, get coffee, make photocopies or plan company parties. By allowing a woman to do this all by herself, you are perpetuating the stereotype that it is a professional woman's role to nurture. Men wrongly assume that women volunteer for these tasks, when, in reality, they are often 'voluntold.' In an HBR article entitled, *Women of Colour Get Asked to Do More 'Office Housework;' Here's How They Can Say No,* Ruchika Tulshyan shares research that shows women of colour are more likely to be assigned or asked to take on office housework tasks, such as ordering lunch or running mentoring programs. Often, women would rather invest their time in high value, strategic work, so wherever you can, help distribute the office housework equally. Even better, choose a task and complete it yourself to demonstrate leadership in changing gender norms at the workplace.

MENTOR

As a leading provider of training and coaching programs, Wet Cement commissioned a research study to assess people's experiences at work through the lens of the company's five Fearless Fundamentals: communication, confidence, connections, courage and control. Their team of behavioural scientists from Wharton, Yale and Cornell University polled 260 mid-level managers across industry sectors with both qualitative and quantitative questions. The study revealed that mentoring is a critical factor in career growth, yet only one in five managers had a mentor and only 34 percent of male respondents mentor others compared to just 25 percent of women. Jennifer Willey, founder and CEO of Wet Cement (and my partner in the Career Excel Women's Leadership Program) advises this, 'Typically, women seek out other women to mentor them or serve as *peer mentors* at work, but this is a big mistake. Men can be the most supportive allies, mentors and sponsors. They can also share how others perceive women in the company (and you specifically). Historically, men hold more power in the workplace, so when they are part of your inner circle, they become valuable advocates who can help shatter gender inequity.'

Authors of *Good Guys* similarly note that mentors can be valuable cultural insiders who understand the dominant culture but have an outsider, non-dominant perspective. Even though some issues are endemic to women within certain cultures, the survey for my book, *Her Way To The Top*, showed sufficient evidence that many challenges working women face are global in nature. Universally, women contend with deep-rooted systemic challenges that impede career success. As a mentor and ally, you can help them confront their feelings, navigate confusion, and overcome obstacles or limiting beliefs. For many maturing girls, confidence begins to erode and self-doubt creeps in—a condition that later negatively impacts their professional lives too. Allies can play an important role in combating social conditioning that severely limits the potential of young women. You may wish to find opportunities to mentor women of all ages in your field, but particularly women who are just starting their careers.

Augmenting the pressure and overwhelming nature of the current Covid-19 crisis, many women who have lost their jobs do not have the skills, nor the technology, to work from home or retrain for other employment. As highlighted earlier, following outbreaks, women experience more irreconcilable work breaks than men do. Hence, it is important to prioritise and direct women to resilience training and corporate development programs that can improve leadership skills. Encourage women to be self-reliant and manage their own finances.

It is equally important to help women contextualise career impediments and identify whether they are system-based or self-imposed, personal limiting beliefs. To tackle external challenges, we need to get our own house in order first. Women are accustomed to traditional female modes of communication, which often underpin compliance and modesty. In the Presidential debate, when Kamala Harris said, 'I am speaking,' every woman who has ever been talked over could identify with her frustration. Mentors can help women normalise Impostor Syndrome feelings, firmly say NO, use more authoritative language to reaffirm versus diminish authority, delegate more, freely disagree, claim their space, ask for more and to be less critical of themselves. Women have a propensity to question their abilities and minimise their achievements, especially in the presence of others. They often put themselves down before others can.

When starting any mentoring relationship, it is useful to set boundaries and establish clear expectations and guidelines regarding availability, communications, meetings and deadlines. Many of the strategies I shared earlier, particularly in relation to questioning and listening, are relevant in this regard. Be mindful not to mould a mini protégé or version of yourself! Encourage the women you mentor to lead their own way which may not necessarily be your way. Remember, it's not about you—it's about them. Be sure your guidance is grounded in what's most beneficial for your mentee. Sometimes, that might entail advising them to consider opportunities outside the existing workplace.

The most valuable mentors trust the expertise of their mentees, encourage their creativity and resourcefulness, and leverage careful questioning to help mentees identify solutions on their own. Of course, there will likely be many occasions when sharing your experience and offering advice is warranted, especially if you feel the mentee has hit a growth roadblock and needs help overcoming it. After all, as a mentor you are expected to be a trusted confidant, who is non-judgmental and will, when required, provide advice and guidance, too. Other times, you will be only be listening to them vent.

As mentors we may sometimes get possessive with our mentees but avoid falling for that trap; ensure they have access to a large pool of diverse mentors and coaches. If you feel that you aren't the right person for this job, then be honest and direct the mentee to someone who is more aligned with their aspirations, values and goals. Some organisations support women's leadership programs that include men, so men are more aware of the challenges their female counterparts face. If you get the opportunity to join one, do so and open yourself up to new perspectives that can help your relationships thrive both personally and professionally. During a crisis, women and marginalised groups are twice as likely to be more vulnerable. It is especially important to advocate for these colleagues and offer them the mentorship they need during these challenging times.

GIVE CONSTRUCTIVE FEEDBACK

I often tell my female coachees to substantiate their promotion request with evidence of their performance and advocate for themselves. I advise them to prepare their 'asks' in advance, convert requests into statements and furnish supporting data that will validate their case. Most bosses are too busy figuring out the most equitable project allocation. Those team members who can vocalise which opportunities and projects they prefer are always considered first. Many senior leaders advanced to their level by weighing facts and figures, so it's important women equip themselves with information that demonstrates their strengths. But, how can women effectively do this if they receive vague feedback that leaves them unaware of the quantifiable impact of their work?

Researchers at Stanford University's Clayman Institute for Gender Research point out that a primary reason why more women are not in senior leadership positions is because they do not receive enough specific feedback tied to outcomes or bottom-line results. Women I mentor and coach share this frustration. Researchers also discovered gender differences within performance reviews, specifically in the language used. When women were praised, they were twice as likely to receive feedback on team contributions versus individual accomplishments. Women were described as supportive, collaborative, and helpful twice as often as men, but those same women were also described as aggressive. Male reviews, on the other hand, included words such as drive, transform, innovate, and tackle. The language used to describe men was less subjective and included highly valued traits. Women received constructive criticism that focused on emotions, personality and tone, while men benefited from more concrete, direct and actionable reviews that clearly highlight the business impact of their projects.

'Stereotypes shape our perceptions of competence. We hold women to a higher standard in evaluations, and women also tend to evaluate themselves to a higher bar,' according to Caroline Simard, director of research at the Clayman Institute. Such hidden biases could ultimately lead to 'cumulative disadvantage over a woman's career over time, resulting in lower access to key leadership positions and stretch assignments, advancement and pay,' Simard concludes.

Sometimes, men are reluctant to give candid feedback and engage in 'protective hesitation' as they are afraid of how a woman will react to harsh criticism. Thus men temper the message so it sounds more considerate, more acceptable. However, in doing so you are failing to fuel their growth because you are focusing on what women want to hear versus what they need to hear. Empathy matters—but authenticity does too. You may want to consider offering this constructive feedback privately versus publicly, so that others do not consider public disagreement as an excuse to undermine her authority. But it is nevertheless crucial to provide insightful developmental feedback which is linked to business goals. This would include specifics about where they need to build skills and which technical projects they could target next. Furthermore, reviews for all employees should be of equal length.

Similarly, ethnic minorities receive extra scrutiny, which leads to less favourable or constructive performance reviews, lower wages and even job loss that prevents them from moving into more visible roles. Individuals from under-represented groups are also penalised for not looking like leaders. As Karen Caitlin writes in *Better Allies*, 'Without quality feedback, members of marginalised groups will find it hard to penetrate the upper echelons of workplace power.'

SHOWCASE FEMALE ROLE MODELS

A recent Grey Area survey revealed one key factor that could influence change—having role models. Role models within an organisation help set the tone for acceptable behaviour and inclusivity. Many women and people of colour miss having many role models to look up to. Female role models from diverse backgrounds in strong leadership positions give a powerful signal that all women can progress within that organisation and that gender, faith or race is no barrier to success. However, it is important to remember that role models are successful on their own terms, not because they have had to compromise themselves to succeed. Barry Boffy from the British Transport Police says, 'Effectively, how much has this individual had to conform to the expectations of an organisation, or its culture, in order to get to the top? This compliance/adjustment/conformity can be equally damaging to women's progression, or the perceived ability to succeed within that organisation. Seeing a woman having to sacrifice elements of herself to conform to the homogeneity—to fit in—sends the message that you actually may not be able to have it all after all.'

As highlighted earlier, women, especially those at the top, have increasingly adopted a macho paradigm and resisted exposing emotion. Other under-represented communities have also come to believe that they must often round their edges to fit into a pre-formed mould and that can be counter-intuitive. As an ally, encourage increased visibility of diverse role models. This will embolden others to bring their true selves to the table, which in turn promotes authentic confidence.

SPONSOR WOMEN

It is not fun being the only *type* in the room, whether it is due to gender, faith, ethnicity or another characteristic; the experience can be isolating. As an ally and sponsor who is willing to take the first few steps towards conscious inclusion, your efforts will help propel women forward in the long run. Instead of feeling ashamed or guilty because you are privileged, use your privilege to advocate for undermined colleagues who deserve recognition for their accomplishments. You can also help them gain perspective and broker connections they need to take on larger roles and advance their careers by providing them with insider, cultural knowledge. Elissa Sangter, Executive Director of The Forte Foundation, encourages women to articulate their career goals to help dictate their own narrative. If you are well positioned or networked, you can support women to do just that and more. Create visibility for them, support/nominate their promotions, provide them with opportunities for professional development, and introduce them to important stakeholders and networks.

Talented women often do not receive credit for their work and they are hesitant to promote their accomplishments, so publicly recognising their performance and offering emphatic endorsements goes a long way toward building their esteem. Invite them to key meetings and recommend them for visible assignments. Keep an eye out for any lacklustre or half-hearted introductions for women, and if you hear it happening, step in to properly introduce them. Sing their praises to others, give them public shout-outs, make referrals and offer meaningful connections.

When I attended university, my college professor Zafar Aziz Osmani, who also worked as Vice President at a major bank, routinely introduced students to opportunities and projects that would raise their profile. He would often talk up our contributions to fellow industry leaders and praise our talent profusely. And he still does that to date. That experience and exposure from a trusted mentor gave my confidence and communication skills a boost early on. Another ally of mine, Neville Gaunt, who has a very strong following on Twitter, frequently tweets about my projects and achievements, which has noticeably boosted their visibility on social media.

Women often miss out on stretch assignments given their own socialised reticence and self-promotion gap. They are often afraid to step up for opportunities due to the fear of rejection and/ or limiting Imposter Syndrome beliefs that they are not 'good enough' for the task. In most of my public and private sector talks, Impostor Syndrome and lack of self-advocacy are always leading challenges for women. As *Good Guys* points out, women also suffer from 'risky investment' bias—managers are often reluctant to take a chance on them and can wrongly assume their lack of interest in the position. If, and when, they do become pregnant, prevent them from being 'mummy-tracked' by discussing entry and exit points that inform a career plan.

As a sponsor ally for a woman, do not wait until she feels ready to nominate her for stretch assignments. When you do launch her into these bigger opportunities, challenge her, encourage her and push her, building her confidence along the way, even if the scope of work is not within her current purview. Women tend to be perfectionists so reinforcing that sometimes 'good enough' is okay can be helpful and much needed!

Avoid micromanaging but be there to provide support in the background, lest challenging assignments become benign sabotage. Back her up based on her potential, not just her performance; this will really expand her development and boost her self-confidence.

Finally, relegating women to certain industries and roles further reinforces bias that there is work naturally suited to men. Sponsoring women for the latter will help challenge stereotypes.

BE AWARE OF MENTAL HEALTH AND LEAD WITH EMPATHY

Covid-19 has had a devastating impact on nearly everyone, particularly in terms of mental health. As an ally, you can encourage regular conversations around mental and physical wellbeing. Keep an eye on the mood and energy levels of female colleagues who may be exhausted from pandemic pressures and excessive workload at home. Watch how their attitude manifests in their behaviour. Do they look eager or are they showing signs of lethargy and apathy?

You can also invite them to an informal one-to-one conversation. Be warm and open so that they feel comfortable enough to open up as well. As an ally who may also be a team leader, set an example by taking sick days/family leave yourself and encourage your team to go home and rest if they appear ill.

Isolation has also led to an alarming uptick in domestic violence. Thousands of women already lack access to resources, hotlines and shelters. Allies can play a key role in directing colleagues to services they need, including domestic violence hotlines, and health and wellbeing contacts and referrals.

Also, encourage people to look out for their colleagues and spot signs if someone is ill or struggling at work. Be empathetic and considerate. A massive workload or strict deadlines can significantly impact time off so continuously reassess priorities. During the pandemic, we have faced an exceptional crisis during which other family members have been working from home too, as are home-schooled children, so the usual dynamics of remote work may not apply. Be flexible when possible. The logistics of working from home while juggling childcare duties leaves many parents feeling challenged, especially mothers. Creating frequent touch points can keep the team connected and engaged so no one member slides off track during the transition period. However, avoid micro-managing and/or over-communicating in such challenging circumstances. Make a list of people you manage and review that list frequently to ensure that everyone's voice is heard in virtual meetings.

Keeping bonds strong and fostering team cohesion virtually is not easy. Employees may be experiencing burnout and given the distraction, uncertainty and overwhelm, they may often be unaware that they are slipping away. Encourage those working with you to take time out for themselves, whether it is for self-care or leisure activities that invigorate them during this stressful time. Begin meetings with open-ended questions—allow people to vent and exchange their thoughts and feelings. It is critical to nurture and strengthen team morale. Introducing virtual water-coolers may also help your team find comfort in their shared human experiences.

Additionally, a robust benefits program that offers discounted healthcare, financial and health advice as well as including resources for emotional, financial and physical wellbeing can really boost productivity.

RESPECT THEIR SPACE AND AVOID USING DIMINUTIVE LANGUAGE

Men who offer women a respectful physical distance, either at work or online, are highly regarded. Pictures of Keanu Reeves with his fans took the Internet by storm when he used the 'hover hand.' The outpouring of support and appreciation indicated that respect for personal space is valued across cultures. Allies acknowledge a woman's need for physical autonomy and understand that it may be inappropriate to hug or touch her without permission. Some women, owing to cultural norms or their own individual preferences, may require a large personal space when men approach them. Survivors of sexual assault or domestic violence are more sensitive to proximity; infringing their personal space can be especially terrifying.

An ally actively avoids and discourages his peers from using pejorative terms such as 'love,' 'dear,' or 'hon' to address colleagues. Nicknames can water down a woman's authority, even if they are unintentional slights. Calling women by 'endearing' names is often offensive so be aware of these common faux pas.

CHOOSE LEADERS WISELY

Sexual harassment, unconscious bias and diversity without leadership support have unintended consequences. History shows us that people in powerful positions can abuse that power. Even though courageous women have stepped forward to share their experiences as victims, not everyone has the strength and opportunity to expose themselves in this way. If you are low in the pecking order, afraid of losing your job or just an employee without a 'media mouthpiece' to amplify and support your case, then your opportunity for justice is severely diminished. It is therefore important to structure significant consequences for the perpetrators of this type of behaviour. But before that, you need to first hire the right leaders.

Leadership consultant Cindy Wahler PhD believes that it is critical to hire leaders who demonstrate respect, exhibit altruism and display compassion, 'Leaders must reinforce behaviours that represent the highest form of integrity and ethics. All leaders must be cognisant of their power and use their influence in positive ways. To do any less, and even worse, is to abuse that power which is a vagrant disregard for humankind.'

As an ally, you can play an important role in choosing the right people as these very people will one day lead the company and set the tone for organisational culture.

SEXIST HUMOUR: AVOID IT BUT DO NOT IGNORE IT

How often have you laughed off a silly infantile joke? We are all guilty of that. We have all heard or shared sexist jokes under the guise of light-hearted banter. According to the *disposition theory of humour*, in the report *Gender, attitudes towards women, and the appreciation of sexist humour,* females should enjoy female-disparaging jokes less than male-disparaging jokes because the recipient of the disparagement in the former situation is a member of the respondent's reference group. However, several studies quoted in this report indicate that both men and women often prefer female-disparaging humour. Sometimes these types of jokes go too far. I recently saw rape memes casually shared across social media platforms after a horrific rape made the national news. Recipients of this content who stay silent are tacitly endorsing it, thus they are part of the problem too.

Sometimes small and seemingly harmless jokes and banter can snowball into truly ugly things that support the larger culture, which normalises disparaging, sexualising and objectifying women. If you view this content with callousness or apathy, it's time to shake things up and avoid being an unintentional perpetrator, or worse still, a silent complicit. In the next section, we will review how to effectively confront people and call them out. 'Boys will be boys' is no excuse for distasteful humour that seeks to ridicule an entire social group. Ben Hurst, campaigner against toxic masculinity, rejects this common phrase as a 'get-out-of-jail free' card for men of all ages. Instead, he notes that 'boys will be what we teach them to be.' A few years ago, video footage surfaced of politicians in a locker room bragging about sexually harassing women. In her article, *Locker Room Talk Isn't Harmless; It Normalises Rape*, author Jaclyn Friedman argues that words matter—joking about harming women plays into a larger narrative where it's okay to progress from words to deeds. She adds, 'Men who boast about hurting women don't often even recognise that's what they're doing, because they see women as instruments for male pleasure and power, not as fully independent human beings.'

Researchers in a publication, *What Did He Mean By That?*

Humour Decreases Attributions of Sexism and Confrontation of Sexist Jokes, discovered that when a sexist remark is delivered as a joke, the humour decreased perceptions that the speaker was sexist, and ultimately decreased the probability that the listener would confront the perpetrator. Alarmingly, hostile sexists were less likely to be confronted when their message was delivered with humour. Sexist, humorous messages actually increased tolerance for sexual harassment in the workplace. Raunchy jokes/lewd humour that demeans or targets women and other minority groups is dangerous for company culture. Men often causally deliver jokes or banter with a punchline and a knowing grin, but that does not make their words any less damaging.

Whether it is locker room talk, a boys' club or any other exclusionist environment, groups of men who reference women in a degrading manner and believe sexist comments give them clout are indirectly propagating rape culture (a perverse culture where men are conditioned to treat women as sex objects). It is long overdue to end it. Once you stop entertaining this kind of male frivolity and show zero tolerance for such belittling and condescending humour, the perpetrators will stop too! Justin Baldoni, actor, filmmaker and social entrepreneur who has been doubling down on his efforts to start a dialogue with men to redefine masculinity, challenges men in his famous *TED Talk: Why I'm done trying to be man enough.* He asks, 'Are you confident enough to listen to the women in your life? To hear their ideas and their solutions? To hold their anguish and actually believe them, even if what they're saying is against you? And will you be man enough to stand up to other men when you hear locker room talk, when you hear stories of sexual harassment? When you hear your boys talking about grabbing ass or getting her drunk, will you actually stand up and do something so that one day we don't have to live in a world where a woman has to risk everything and come forward to say the words me too?'

UNDERSTAND HOW SEXUAL HARASSMENT IMPACTS WOMEN

Sexual harassment is largely considered a women's issue even though the issue itself lies with men, or rather, exists as a manifestation of a misogynist society. Yet, the burden of fighting sexual harassment or any form of gender violence seems to fall indiscriminately on women's shoulders when it should, in fact, be an issue that men help solve. That burden includes legal action, enforcing policy, and building awareness for an issue that permeates many office cultures.

When reading the book, someone asked me if it was necessary to highlight this topic here in more detail. So here is the thing— whether it's work or any other place, feeling safe is not a luxury automatically afforded to women. We often have to fight for it even in the least suspecting environments (work included) so yes, this is necessary.

The majority of women and girls in the UK have experienced sexual harassment in public places, according to new data from UN Women. The study found that 97 percent of women aged 18 to 24 have experienced sexual harassment in public spaces, and more than 70 percent of women of all ages have endured such behaviour. The data was collected from a YouGov survey of more than 1,000 women commissioned in January 2021 by UN Women UK. The research also showed a lack of faith in authorities, with just four percent of women telling YouGov they had reported incidents of harassment to an official organisation, and 45 percent of women stating they didn't believe reporting it would change anything. 'This is a human rights crisis. It's just not enough for us to keep saying "this is too difficult a problem for us to solve;" it needs addressing now,' Claire Barnett, executive director of UN Women UK told The Guardian newspaper.

In recent years, the #MeToo campaign has unleashed a barrage of global emotions and protests. The Harvey Weinstein and Jeffrey Epstein scandals, and the more recent tragic case of Sarah Everard, have highlighted the challenges women have historically faced in trying to address sexual harassment and attempting to protect themselves. Figures published by the government's Office for National Statistics (ONS) after Sarah Everards's case revealed that in England and Wales, fewer than one in six women and one in five men report crimes of sexual assault to the police. The ONS figures also showed adults of Black and mixed ethnicity were more likely to experience sexual assault. Welsh government adviser Yasmin Khan who founded the Halo Project—a support network for abused ethnic minority women and girls, in an interview with Al Jazeera—said police discrimination is leaving minority victims of sexual abuse particularly out in the cold.

People have since stepped up to express outrage in solidarity with victims; it's a sign that we are definitely heading in the right direction. But we need to do more as a society, especially since the global pandemic has exacerbated gender violence. I honestly believe only a handful of girls or women in this entire world will have avoided some form of harassment in their lifetime, be it explicit or implicit. Unfortunately, some women experience far worse scenarios than others. Whether it's an inappropriate touch in a public place, men purposefully brushing past you, an indecent prolonged stare, or an inappropriate comment or conversation that makes you uncomfortable—WE ALL have been there one way or another!

Moreover, there are men of every race, religion and socioeconomic status who rape or sexually harass women, but news coverage often blames women for the assault. The victim's appearance and sexual history are called into question, instead of the perpetrator's actions. As an ally, you will first and foremost, avoid claiming false meritocracy and denying that this has happened in your own workplace.

Harassment can be physical, verbal and/or non-verbal. It can happen to anyone in any environment and it can be either a one-off or series of incidents. A critical measure of the offence is how the behaviour makes the victim feel. The European Community Code of Practice describes it as, 'unwanted or unwelcome conduct of a sexual nature, or other conduct based on sex, affecting the dignity of women and men at work. This can include unwelcome physical, verbal, or non-verbal conduct.'

According to Louisa Symington-Mills, CEO of City Mothers and City Fathers, 'No one should have to endure such behaviour in the workplace—or anywhere else. Behaviour that is unwelcome and intimidating can transform an office environment from harmonious to odious, and can have immediate impact on the health and happiness of the victim, as well as the wellbeing of those that work closely with her.' Louisa adds that whether or not a comment or action is inappropriate is a subjective determination, but if you are upset and uncomfortable as a result, then it's an indicator of harassment. The sad part is that it can be easy to trivialise sexual harassment—particularly when you compare it to more severe forms of sexual assault. A leery look on the street isn't as bad as actually being grabbed, right? Women therefore choose to ignore comparatively smaller or insignificant forms of harassment like micro-aggressions, because thank God, at least nobody touched or groped them. That would have been far more traumatising, so they learn to stay quiet about an incident that isn't a big deal, even if it is!

There are two types of sexual harassment:

- **Quid Pro Quo: In** Latin, this phrase translates into 'this for that.' For example, an employer commits to giving an employee this job, this promotion, or this benefit, for that sexual favour.
- **Hostile Environment:** This type of harassment is more difficult to identify. It occurs when harassing behaviour creates an unfriendly, negative work environment for an employee.

Many harassers use excuses to vindicate themselves, such as:

- **She laughed at my joke so I thought she didn't mind.** Some employees feel obligated to participate or laugh for fear of being negatively judged, but just because she smiled it doesn't mean she is not uncomfortable.
- **It happened on a business trip, so it doesn't count.** Whether it took place in or outside the office, it does not change the context. It is still harassment, wherever it occurs.
- **It was just a compliment.** Compliments that make someone else uneasy fall under harassment too.
- **It only happened once.** Whether it occurred once or 20 times, it is still harassment.
- **The comments were directed at someone else.** If you witness inappropriate comments (such as your colleague commenting on how someone else might be in bed, without that person present) you can still file a sexual harassment complaint.

- **Sexual harassment is all about sex, and sex didn't happen**. Inappropriate touching and either direct or indirect verbal harassment still counts.
- **This is the way I've grown up; you can't expect me to change.** Other employees are not expected to accommodate and adjust to what you think is socially acceptable or *normal*.

A common defence in harassment-related claims is that the victim 'asked for it' given her choice of clothing, make-up, etc. Victim blaming gives some men a free pass to blatantly violate ethical and moral boundaries and sidestep responsibility. Another common discrediting tactic is questioning the delay in reporting a crime, the 'Why did she wait so long to expose the crime if she didn't enjoy it?' query.

Consider that a woman who is harassed or attacked is no different from any other victim of an attack. When an animal attacks (i.e. a dog bites a human) do people question why the victim didn't immediately respond to that animal or show displeasure? Most people have a fright or flight response. Many victims may freeze on the spot, then struggle with feelings of shame, disgust and confusion that cloud their judgment. Most feel so disoriented by the violation that that they do not have the capacity to talk about the incident until much later on once they have processed what has happened. But sometimes, the damage cuts deeper than shame or humiliation; victims can develop post-traumatic stress disorder (PTSD) or other mental trauma that prevent them from coming forward. The negative psychological effects of repeated abuse are cumulative and extremely detrimental. And finally, women may be afraid to expose the incident for fear of personal and professional backlash.

The US Merit Systems Protection Board states that unwelcome behaviour can fall into seven categories:

1. Sexual teasing, remarks, jokes or questions.
2. Pressure for dates.
3. Letters, emails, telephone calls, or materials of a sexual nature.
4. Sexual looks or gestures.
5. Deliberate touching, leaning over, cornering or pinching.
6. Pressure for sexual favours.
7. Actual/attempted sexual assault or rape.

Other behaviours include:

1. Displaying inappropriate sexual images or posters in the workplace.
2. Staring in a sexually suggestive or offensive manner, or whistling.
3. Making sexual comments about appearance, clothing or body parts.
4. Inappropriate touching including pinching, patting, rubbing, or purposefully brushing up against another person.
5. Asking sexual questions such as questions about someone's sexual history or sexual orientation.

Some men may justify the use of compliments but often it is not just the words but the accompanying tone and look that make the recipient of any 'compliment' uncomfortable. The Good Men Project describes this aptly: 'Appearance for both men and women is a personal matter. Some put more stock in it than others.

However, women in particular, work to ensure that recognition of their merits has nothing to do with what they look like, but what they have achieved. When you notice superficial things about a woman it is best to keep them to yourself. If you find things admirable and feel compelled to say something, stick to professional achievements. Being recognised for hard work and intelligence is generally well received by women and men alike. And truly, those are the areas that matter.'

At the beginning of my career, my father highlighted an important difference between personal and non-personal gifts that I still consider a useful benchmark when accepting gifts from male colleagues. Personal gifts include anything that comes in contact with your body such as cosmetics, perfume, clothes, accessories etc and many women consider these items to be unacceptable workplace gifts. Non-personal gifts include books, mugs, stationery etc that are more acceptable in the workplace. These classifications may be more of a personal preference, but the purpose is to recognise the difference.

Now, let's review some common arguments, which are often used to undermine and deflect from the main issue.

The 'Hey, But What about the Rest of Us' Argument

Some people in privileged groups may believe they are victims of reverse discrimination or be afraid of the Oppression Olympics trap. These people create a competing narrative when they see others championing marginalised communities or highlighting inequalities. Irrespective of background, gender, ethnicity and faith, everyone matters in an inclusive space, and everyone should be heard. However, I also believe that timing is everything. If you need to raise another issue, raise it respectfully at the proper time, but do not compete for attention during a critical time; it is distasteful and inappropriate. When you offer your condolences to a grieving individual, instead of focusing on his/her loss, do you mention your own deceased family members to earn sympathy? No, right?

All tragedies/injustices should be addressed in their own space, at the proper time and with due attention rather than highlighted in response to another. No atrocities against any victims are justified—we should advocate for all with the exclusive attention each deserves. However, when you draw comparisons or shift the primary focus of a pressing and grave campaign, you are neither healing nor driving positive change.

The '#MeToo Movement Has Made it Difficult For Men' Argument

The study published in Journal Organisational Dynamics, cited earlier, suggests that men are now afraid to be alone with women in the room—so much so that some are even afraid to shake hands so they avoid contact altogether. Ironically, the same research debunks the argument that men are confused about what exactly constitutes unacceptable behaviour. The study examined 19 behaviours including emailing sexual jokes to a subordinate, and asked respondents to classify each as harassment or socially acceptable behaviour. The results showed that both genders essentially agreed on what entails harassment.

'Most men know what sexual harassment is and most women know what it is,' says Leanne Atwater, a professor at the University of Houston and one of the study's authors. 'The idea that men don't know their behaviour is bad and that women are making a mountain out of a molehill is largely untrue. If anything, women are more lenient in defining harassment.'

So if men are aware of unacceptable versus acceptable behaviours, then why are they so afraid? In her article, *Men Now*

Avoid Women at Work–Another Sign We're Being Punished for #MeToo, journalist Arwa Mahdawi writes: 'The answer to that question, perhaps, is that a lot of men aren't so much afraid of being accused of anything as they are angry that #MeToo ever happened. They're angry that they've been made to think about their behaviour, made to interrogate power dynamics they always took for granted, and they are punishing women for it by refusing to interact with them.'

The 'Not All Men' Argument

Following news of Sarah Everard's disappearance and her appalling murder, national and international conversations and protests were triggered like never before. Social media witnessed an outpouring of support, hundreds of men stepped up and asked how they could help women feel safer at night. However, at the same time the hashtag #NotAllMen started trending, as it typically does when women become victims of male violence, and this irked and saddened many. 'Not all men are like that' sounds defensive. Just like #AllLivesMatter side-tracks an important conversation, this response suggests you are not listening to the issue and are more focused on protecting yourself. As Sian Lewis, Associate Lecturer in Criminology and Sociology, University of Roehampton notes, the response insinuates you are more concerned with how this situation impacts you as a man or your entire social group versus the wellbeing of the woman who was harassed or assaulted.

Women already know that not all men are rapists or abusers. They don't need you to tell them that. However, when a woman walks alone in the street or navigates any public space, she wouldn't necessarily know which category you fall into–she will automatically feel threated if an unknown man starts walking next to her because it's a natural instinct. In Karachi and Dubai,

I never dared to, but on the few occasions in London that I have walked home alone at night from the train station, every single time, I have experienced palpitations, particularly if I sensed a stranger walking next to me or felt that I was not alone. Nearly every woman who has ever walked alone at night has been fearful of what might befall her.

Also, consider this parallel argument: during Covid-19 the government advised everyone to stay home. Many people are sick and the virus is spreading fast. You respond, 'Yes, but not everyone is infected.' Whether everyone is sick or just a few individuals, you must take precautions either way. So yes—not all men behave like that—yet enough of them do, which is why women are conditioned to be on guard all of the time.

Jackson Katz, a social researcher, asked men and women what they did on a daily basis to avoid being sexually assaulted. The results of the research, as shared on social media, evidenced a stark contrast between the response of men, who had nothing to bother about, and the women, whose list of precautions could go on forever. This doesn't mean that men never had any safety concerns at all, it only points out how the fear and threat of sexual assault is predominantly a woman's issue.

Jameela Jamil, an English TV and radio presenter, put a post on Instagram in response to #NotAllMen trending hashtag following Sarah Everard's untimely death. Her message resonated with many. She wrote, 'It's true that #notallmen harm women, but do all men work to make sure their fellow men do not harm women? Do they interrupt troubling language and behaviour in others? Do they have conversations about women's safety/consent with their sons? Are #allmen interested in our safety? You don't get to exclude yourself from the wrong side unless you're actively fighting on the right side.'

The 'But Men Are Victims Too' Argument

Recognising that women are disproportionately affected by sexual violence does not deny that men and boys are also victims of sexual violence. The stigma and shame of male survivors is more aggravated by toxic masculinity. These men need their own space and activism. However, counter campaigns and retaliatory movements hardly help.

Claiming the issue is gender neutral only undermines the severity and impact that sexual harassment and abuse have on women's everyday lives. Even worse, sexist men use this sentiment not to defend victimised men, but rather discredit a prevalent issue.

The 'Why Didn't You Tell Him Off?' Argument

Telling someone how to behave, mislaying the blame and playing devil's advocate are other forms of victim blaming. It feeds into the dangerous narrative that it is a woman's responsibility to keep herself safe from men—that she must alter her behaviour to exist in a world where sexual harassment is normalised and thus inevitable. This shift of responsibility and lack of ownership is exhausting for women. It invalidates their experiences and silences their voices. As Sian Lewis, notes in an article, 'It doesn't take much to listen, but it can make all the difference to how a story is told.'

As an ally, it is important to do what is right for the victim versus protecting the interests of the organisation. Many corporate HR departments are not supportive and focus on avoiding legal action at any cost. As an ally, it is critical for you to lend support, help victims channel their inner strength and ensure confidentiality and trust. You may also suggest appointing a designated third party or victim's advocate who is impartial and fair. Training on acceptable and unacceptable behaviours, creating a sexual harassment policy in collaboration with HR and D&I consultants, and conducting exit interviews/surveys are some measures to alleviate harassment. You could also review policies, procedures and practices to identify loopholes, establish accountability, develop a proper complaint procedure and push for a broader cultural change in the organisation.

UNDERSTAND CONSENT

It is important to understand the meaning of consent and actively initiate and engage in discussions that explore what consent means to those around you, including children. The concept of consent is still quite muddy and people often take advantage of the blurred lines to support their own agenda.

Former schoolgirl and sexual abuse survivor, Soma Sara, 22, sparked a #MeToo movement in UK schools with her website www.everyonesinvited.uk @advancingyou, which has seen the number of testimonials being shared skyrocket since the female safety movement was triggered by the Sarah Everard tragedy. The website lifts the lid on a collection of horrifying stories from young teenagers pressured into harassment, assault and rape. Many of top independent institutions have been named and the stories make for grim reading. Girls as young as 11 say they've been molested in front of cheering pupils in parks, amongst other appalling incidents. These nasty, spine-chilling revelations of rape culture in schools support the dire need to teach children how to combat coercion and recognise the true meaning of consent.

It's sad and shocking how most women are already well aware of the persistent culture of toxic masculinity in schools. Since 2013, Deana Puccio and her co-founder Allison Havey have been running The RAP Project, which holds workshops about rape and sexual assault in schools. Many of the questions these women are asked in these sessions are concerning, for example:

- If a girl comes back to my house, doesn't she want it?
- If she dresses and acts a certain way and is drinking, doesn't she want it?
- If a girl has passed out after drinking alcohol but mumbles 'yes', is that consent?

Their workshops also cover hardcore porn and the fact that boys younger than 11 are being manipulated by the industry, which is trying to get them addicted to it. Puccio notes, 'What surprises me most is when you ask them what consent is, they answer: it means 16 years old.'

It's now more important than ever that children be taught about respect and consent so they carry this understanding forward into adulthood. This education should occur both in school and at home. Schools have started holding lessons, talks and assemblies; children have also engaged in valuable focus group discussions. Although boys can feel naturally defensive, afraid or guilty, there is also a positive leaning-in.

Everyonesinvited.uk has issued a statement on its website urging the community to practice empathy and calling for reconciliation by 'forgiving and [going] forward.' This feeling is being reflected in classrooms.

To fully understand the concept of consent and teach it to your children, I recommend watching Emmeline May's tea analogy video. The underlying message of this creative campaign is that sex without consent is rape.

Consentiseverything.com details specific conditions for those that are unclear. And even though the analogy includes some caveats, it does clarify the issue and help spread awareness with a wider audience.

Here is the tea analogy (included with permission from Emmeline May, 2014). Transcript of the analogy has been extracted from her blog published in the Huffington Post.

Consent: Not Actually That Complicated
Huffington Post

'If you're still struggling, just imagine instead of initiating sex, you're making them a cup of tea. You say 'hey, would you like a cup of tea?' and they go 'omg f*** yes, I would f*****g LOVE a cup of tea! Thank you!' then you know they want a cup of tea.'

'If you say 'hey, would you like a cup of tea?' and they um and ahh and say, 'I'm not really sure...' then you can make them a cup of tea or not, but be aware that they might not drink it, and if they don't drink it then - this is the important bit - don't make them drink it. You can't blame them for you going to the effort of making the tea on the off-chance they wanted it; you just have to deal with them not drinking it. Just because you made it doesn't mean you are entitled to watch them drink it.'

'If they say 'No thank you' then don't make them tea. At all. Don't make them tea, don't make them drink tea, don't get annoyed at them for not wanting tea. They just don't want tea, ok?'

'They might say, 'Yes please, that's kind of you' and then when the tea arrives they actually don't want the tea at all. Sure, that's kind of annoying as you've gone to

---

the effort of making the tea, but they remain under no obligation to drink the tea. They did want tea, now they don't. Sometimes people change their mind in the time it takes to boil that kettle, brew the tea and add the milk. And it's okay for people to change their mind, and you are still not entitled to watch them drink it even though you went to the trouble of making it.'

'If they are unconscious, don't make them tea. Unconscious people don't want tea and can't answer the question, 'do you want tea' because they are unconscious.'

'Okay, maybe they were conscious when you asked them if they wanted tea, and they said yes, but in the time it took you to boil that kettle, brew the tea and add the milk they are now unconscious. You should just put the tea down, make sure the unconscious person is safe, and - this is the important bit - don't make them drink the tea. They said yes then, sure, but unconscious people don't want tea.'

'If someone said yes to tea, started drinking it, and then passed out before they'd finished it, don't keep on pouring it down their throat. Take the tea away and make sure they are safe. Because unconscious people don't want tea. Trust me on this.'

'If someone said 'yes' to tea around your house last Saturday, that doesn't mean that they want you to make them tea all the time. They don't want you to come around unexpectedly to their place and make them tea and force them to drink it going 'BUT YOU WANTED TEA LAST WEEK,' or to wake up to find you pouring tea down their throat going, 'BUT YOU WANTED TEA LAST NIGHT.''

'Do you think this is a stupid analogy? Yes, you all know this already - of course you wouldn't force feed someone tea because they said yes to a cup last week. Of COURSE you wouldn't pour tea down the throat of an unconscious person because they said yes to tea five minutes ago when they were conscious. But if you can understand how completely ludicrous it is to force people to have tea when they don't want tea, and you are able to understand when people don't want tea, then how hard is it to understand when it comes to sex?'

'Whether it's tea or sex, Consent Is Everything.'

'And on that note, I am going to make myself a cup of tea.'

After the video's release, some additional comments suggest that if you have consented to tea being served in a cup—and only in a cup—and it comes in a mug, then consent has not been given. People have also similarly pointed out that the video needs to consider how youth, disability or a head injury (which can impact judgement and decision making) may lead to abuse of trust.

SUMMARY

Educate Yourself

You cannot change or address what you are not aware of. Make an effort to be cognisant of issues impacting under-represented groups and how these challenges may have been exacerbated by the pandemic. At this point, it might also be useful to get some clarity on what you actually want to achieve on your allyship journey and think about which benefits specifically appeal to you.

Recognise Privilege

When you belong to a privileged or powerful group, you do not need to draw attention to yourself as a specific entity because you have status. What's more, others perceive you as the standard versus an outlier. But when you belong to an under-represented group, the 'usual' dynamics shift—it's important to be wary of those dynamics. Being a member of a privileged group does not mean you never struggled; it simply means you haven't faced the same impediments that others may have faced. Pay special attention to intersectionality challenges.

Be Transparent and Authentic

Reach out to colleagues, be as transparent as you can, and share what you know while being honest about what you don't know. And if there's any miscommunication, rectify and apologise—spare the audacity—people will acknowledge genuine intent more than a half-hearted cover-up. Also, don't assume you know what's best.

Ask

The only way to become an ally 'in the know' is to ask the right questions. The more you know, the easier it will become to help colleagues feel more comfortable. That said, how you ask is as important as what you ask. You do not want to sound intrusive, just naturally curious and genuinely interested in finding out answers. Surveys and polls can help build awareness. Another effective method is to create opportunities for women by establishing networks to share grievances.

Listen
Active listening involves making a conscious effort to hear and understand the message while being conscious of the non-verbal aspects of the conversation. Physical indicators include making eye contact, nodding your head from time to time, and leaning into the conversation. You can also give verbal cues or use phrases such as 'Uh-huh,' 'Go on,' 'Really!' and 'Then what?'

Prepare to Be Uncomfortable
When you ask questions with the intention to grow, chances are you will receive unexpected feedback that might be awkward, even unpleasant. As human beings, we are wired to react when attacked, but don't give in to that urge. Self-awareness, but more importantly, self-control, are important to develop gender empathy.

Acknowledge Your Responsibility
Everyone occasionally commits a faux pas in the workplace, but what matters most is admitting your mistake and learning from it. If you are open to being challenged, also be willing to apologise.

Acknowledge Your Bias
As human beings, we have a natural tendency to judge and form internal biases, but we can unlearn harmful tendencies and behaviours. Questioning yourself can distance you from

debilitating biases and enable you to view situations objectively. You can subvert each bias by testing its validity through a belief-audit that allows you to identify holes in your thinking.

Don't Make Assumptions

Avoid making assumptions about habits, preferences, choices and aptitude based solely on gender. Questions surrounding career choices are far too common for women, and they often receive pushback from others who think they are stepping outside of gender norms. It is common to assume a person's profession based on age, gender or race.

Avoid Stereotyping and Generalising

The racially diverse groups you work with might not fit the stereotypes society defines for that group, so avoid clustering communities and their respective issues. Aspire to understand unique experiences and identities; your advice or questions may not be suited for women of colour or other marginalised groups, so do not offer one-size-fits-all solutions. Pay attention to gender rules that often become unconscious in adulthood but continue to profoundly impact our habits, assumptions and beliefs about how to work, interact and socialise. Be consistent in how you refer to all genders and avoid gender-biased expressions. To avoid discriminatory language, reverse the gender and check whether the meaning or emphasis of the sentence changes or sounds odd. If it's not relevant to the communication, it is best to avoid using gender specific pronouns.

Avoid Undermining Women through These Harmful Practices

Men consciously or unconsciously engage in certain harmful practices that make women and diverse racial groups uncomfortable and can sabotage their confidence. If you are aware of these issues, you are better positioned to call the behaviour out when you spot it.

Engage With Others Outside Your Circle
Expand your social and professional circles. Especially, reach out to people missing from your circle and make an effort to know them personally. Sometimes micro-aggressions occur simply because we are unaware of them.

Believe Her
When women share a grievance, believe what they say without attaching your own assumptions, and assuming positive intent. Even if you are cautious of validating before investigating, it is important to be empathetic.

Be Vigilant
As an ally, it is essential to keep an ear to the ground. Actively scan your environment to spot visibly unhappy or disengaged female colleagues. Colleagues who seem distracted, depressed, or participate/engage less than usual, may be struggling. Networks provide opportunities for colleagues to be vulnerable and share their challenges in a safe space.

Share the Workload at Home
As an ally, you can lighten your partner's workload by sharing household chores. If you are a parent, especially if you are a senior leader, participate in your children's lives, help out with doctor appointments, parent-teacher meetings amd homework, to proactively demonstrate that these tasks are not a mother's responsibility alone. Do not shy away from taking parenting leave to support your partner and divide responsibilities that women traditionally own.

What You Tell Your Children is Important

We already face a long list of challenges due to skewed social conditioning. It is not too late to influence the existing generation and help them think differently. Let's change the dynamics by teaching boys and girls to be responsible, empowered and empathetic individuals who are ready to call out gendered actions or assumptions, hold each other accountable, and positively influence each other's behaviours and beliefs.

Share Office Housework

Women typically take meeting notes, get coffee, make photocopies or plan company parties. Often, women would rather invest their time in higher value strategic work, so wherever you can, distribute the office housework equally. Choose a task and complete it to demonstrate leadership in changing gender norms in the workplace.

Mentor

As a mentor and ally, you can help women confront their feelings, navigate confusion, contextualise career blocks and overcome obstacles or limiting beliefs, amongst other things. But avoid being possessive; ensure they have access to a large pool of diverse mentors and coaches. If you aren't the right person for this job, then be honest and direct the mentee to someone who is more aligned with their aspirations, values and goals.

Give Constructive Feedback

It is crucial to provide female colleagues with insightful developmental feedback that is linked to business goals. This includes specifics about where they need to build skills and which technical projects they could target next. Furthermore, reviews for all employees should be of equal length.

Showcase Female Role Models

Female role models from diverse backgrounds in strong leadership positions give a powerful signal that all women can progress within the organisation and gender, faith and race are not barriers to success. However, it is important to remember that role models are successful on their own terms, not because they have had to compromise themselves to succeed.

Sponsor

Create visibility for women, support/nominate their promotions, provide opportunities for professional development, and introduce them to important stakeholders and networks. Nominate her for stretch assignments. When you do launch her into larger opportunities, challenge her, encourage her and push her, building her confidence along the way even if the scope of work is not within her current purview.

Be Aware of Mental Health and Lead with Empathy

Encourage regular conversations around mental and physical wellbeing. Keep an eye on the mood and energy levels of female colleagues who may be exhausted from pandemic pressures and excessive workload at home. Allies can play a key role in directing colleagues to services they need, including domestic violence hotlines, and health and wellbeing contacts and referrals.

Respect Personal Space and Avoid Using Diminutive Language

Acknowledge a woman's need for physical autonomy and understand that it may be inappropriate to hug or touch her without permission. Some women may prefer a large personal space when men approach them. Survivors of sexual assault or domestic violence are more sensitive to proximity; infringing their personal space can be especially terrifying. Actively avoid, and discourages peers, from using pejorative terms such as, 'love,' 'dear,' or 'hon' to address colleagues.

Choose Leaders Wisely
As an ally, you can play an important role in choosing the right people; these people will one day lead the company and set the tone for organisational culture.

Sexist Humour: Avoid It but Do Not Ignore It
Sometimes small and seemingly harmless jokes and banter can snowball into truly ugly things that support the broader company culture that normalises disparaging, sexualising and objectifying women. If you view this content with callousness or apathy, it's time to shake things up and avoid being an unintentional perpetrator, or worse still, a silent complicit.

Understand How Sexual Harassment Impacts Women
As an ally, it is important to be aware of the context and impact of sexual harassment at work and do what is right for the victim versus protecting the interests of the organisation.

Understand Consent
Understand the meaning of consent and actively initiate and engage in discussions that explore what consent means to those around you, including children. The concept of consent is still quite muddy and people often take advantage of the blurred lines to support their own agenda.

SECTION TWO

CHALLENGE OTHERS

'The ultimate measure of a man is not where he stands in moments of comfort and convenience, but where he stands at times of challenge and controversy.'
-Martin Luther King Jr.-

So far, the onus has been on you, although you may still be processing the strategies offered. However, now comes the more difficult bit when you start confronting others about their behaviour. If the culture in your institution is saturated with bias and sexism, people may hardly notice inappropriate comments. To take on overt sexism by yourself, you may have to regulate conversations and police other people's tone. And that's not exactly a piece of cake. Understandably, this can be awkward plus there is the long-standing 'bro code' that is hard to break.

Good Guys highlights that sometimes even well-intentioned people adopt a passive responsibility—they may give the appearance of taking responsibility, but they are ambivalent, reluctant or flat-out missing when public action or risky advocacy is required. This is referred to as 'bystander apathy' and interestingly enough, research by American scientists Latané and Darley shows that the larger the room and the crowd, the more likely it is there will be diffusion of responsibility. People tend to believe it is better to mind their own business, keep their head down and avoid conflict when it comes to issues of political correctness.

However, it's necessary to challenge violators because sometimes others do not realise their behaviour is inappropriate until someone points it out; when someone from their own circle does the 'pointing,' it also carries more weight. Don't hesitate to identify issues and raise awareness in respectful ways. In fact, be tactful whenever possible. Your willingness to intervene could lead to a transformative change in the workplace. After all, even small acts of resistance can make a difference. According to Samantha Rennie, Former Executive Director at Rosa, 'People must be held accountable for their thoughts and their actions, so when you see acts of sexism, racism, xenophobia, ableism, Islamophobia, or anything else, call it out!'

When a man suggests in a public forum that sexism has occurred and thereby challenges the perpetrators, targets of sexism report greater self-confidence as opposed to women who are often negatively evaluated when they personally report an issue. Moreover, when a man overtly ends an offensive conversation, it changes the atmosphere and observers are more likely to be persuaded.

W. Brad Johnson and David G. Smith further note, 'How a message is received is often less about precise wording and more about the in-group identity of the speaker. A confrontation intended to change attitudes and behaviour has more impact when it comes from someone perceived to be similar—in this case, another man who can claim, "That's not who we [men] are" and "That's not what we [guys] do".'

Failing to publicly call out an incident damages workplace culture because it is a tacit endorsement of inappropriate behaviour. Why wouldn't the pattern continue if no one identifies a problem? Moreover, to reiterate, other men take note when men speak up in defence of women. As an ally, you need to support respectful and inclusive behaviour that fosters a healthy work culture for all. In doing so, you are empowering the next generation of men as a courageous exemplar. As Martin Luther King Jr. rightly said, 'In the end, we will remember not the words of our enemies, but the silence of our friends.'

That said, whether you will call out behaviour/comments publicly or privately depends on a number of things. According to Smith and Johnson, authors of *Good Guys,* if the perpetrator is genuinely misinformed and immature but generally well-intentioned, or if he is from an older generation or culture (one that is possibly out of touch with changing values) consider calling him out privately. Furthermore, if no one was specifically targeted or affected, or if you share a positive relationship with that man that could lead to a productive side discussion, then it is better to address the issue in private. But for someone who is an unapologetic, serial offender who makes a flagrantly inappropriate joke, is old enough to know better, yet remains directly offensive, then you may wish to consider confronting him publicly to help change his behaviour. Smith and Johnson also warn us to be especially attuned to people who say, 'I am not sexist or racist but. . .' and then go on to add an observation. These individuals may be developing insight about bias and sexism, but are still working through the denial stage. As previously noted, labelling someone is unhelpful, as is confronting an offender in a hostile and accusatory manner. Be empathetic but do not let them off the hook. Here are some different ways of calling out others.

CONFRONT PRIVATELY

In choosing to respond, you could do so immediately or wait until you are in more control of your feelings. Listed below are few tips to bear in mind during any private confrontation.

Take Charge of Your Emotions
When you do decide to directly confront an individual, marshal your courage and temper your anxiety, especially if you are not in a leadership role that naturally commands respect and authority or you are calling out someone senior to you. Plan in advance how you will handle the situation and visualise yourself in control. Here are some tips:

- Take a deep breath and relax.
- Tell yourself that getting upset won't help.
- Remind yourself that as long as you keep your cool, you're in control and you will not let them get to you. You will find a way to say what you want to without anger.
- Stay calm—no sarcasm, no attacks, no judgments.
- No matter what is said, know that you are a good person for speaking the truth (men are often shamed for siding with women).
- Anger won't solve anything but staying rational will.

Bullies sense fear and prey on weakness. Show them upfront that you are strong and they will usually back down. Your body language is crucial. Stand up straight, don't fidget, use a calm and collected tone, and maintain eye contact.

Start Positive
Be polite and respectful. Don't aggravate the situation—remain calm and state why a behaviour or comment is offensive. Stick to exactly what has happened and don't exaggerate. For example, 'I

want to let you know how I am feeling because I believe that it will clear the air between us.' You could share an appreciation, but make sure it is sincere. 'Over the past year, I have really enjoyed working with you. However, I've noticed that lately. . .'

Be Direct
Use the first person point of view and say, 'I am [or XYZ] is feeling irritated/annoyed/angry.'

Don't distance yourself from your feelings with impersonal, third-person statements and generalisations such as, 'When people. . .' or, 'it can be annoying when. . .'

Use 'I' messages instead. Also, specify your degree of anger. This can vary from, 'I've been getting slightly irritated,' to 'my fury is reaching the boiling point.'

Sharing this information often helps the other person listen more carefully. If you just say, 'I am angry with you, you may unnecessarily freeze the other person with fright or prompt him/ her into aggressive, defensive behaviour.

Share the Victim's Feelings of Threat and Fear
For example, 'She may be frightened of saying this to you because you might think she is being petty or you may reject her/fire her/ hit her, but. . .' This will help you feel more in control of your feelings and may earn you some welcome and helpful reassurance. For example, they may respond with, 'No, I promise that I will try and listen to what you have to say without walking away or punishing you/her/XYZ.'

Another way of starting the conversation is by stating what you saw and heard without making a judgment, then sharing your opinion of the matter. Finally, disclose what you need or want from the other person to resolve the issue. For example, 'When you continuously interrupt Sara, it seems like she is less likely to contribute to team meetings. She feels disrespected and the rest of us feel uncomfortable. I would like you to let her finish what she is saying.'

Avoid Put Downs and Don't Invite Criticism or Retaliation
Don't say things such as:

- I know that she is a bit of a nag. . .
- She is over-sensitive.
- She is too soft.
- You'll probably scream at me/want to kill me when I tell you. . .

By doing so you are sharing inflammatory ideas, validating the behaviour and unintentionally fanning the flames while confirming harmful gender stereotypes. After you handle a situation, analyse it, learn from it, and then put it aside. If you are still angry afterwards, channel that anger into doing something constructive like organising your office, or calmly remove yourself from the room and go for a walk.

CONFRONT PUBLICLY

If you plan on confronting the aggressor publicly, these examples demonstrate how you can react and/or challenge in respectful ways.

Respond to Offensive Jokes
- I don't get it, can you explain?
- That wasn't funny at all!

- That's against our code of conduct.
- Did you really just say that?
- That's an inappropriate generalisation/stereotype!
- That's not okay!
- We don't do that here!
- That made me uncomfortable!
- Wow, this is inappropriate/awkward!
- I didn't find that joke funny. I don't like how it demeans women!
- Please be mindful when saying this.
- You may want to more careful about your choice of words.
- This is not true.
- Disrespectful words are not tolerated here.

Respond to Social/Physical Harassment

Statements such as, 'Get your hands off her' or 'Stay away from her' are firm, assertive and non-negotiable. Also, 'Is everything okay in here?' 'This behaviour is not acceptable.' 'We don't do that here!'

If you can't directly call out a violator, for whatever reason, you can deploy a distraction or interruption strategy to start a conversation with the perpetrator and allow his potential target to safely exit the scene. You can also help remove the victim from the situation by telling her she needs to take a call, or that you need to speak to her personally; any excuse works to get her to safety. If you are too embarrassed or shy to speak out, or if you don't feel comfortable doing so, ask someone else to step in. Any decent venue has a zero-tolerance policy on harassment, so the staff should be empowered to act.

In any case, do reach out and directly ask the victim later if she is okay and report it when it's safe to do so—it's never too late to act. Below you will find some more strategies to call out any problematic behaviour or comment.

Ask a Reflective Question
'Did you just say Helen is offensive?' Sometimes when you repeat the offensive statement, others retreat or reflect on what they've said and how it might be received. For example, someone says, 'I want Susan to be less bossy' and you may respond by repeating their judgemental word of choice. . .'Bossy?' The reflective question usually prompts an expanded answer so you don't have to ask more questions. For optimal effect, pair your question with a pause.

Pause
Simply stop talking. People often do not like silence and will invariably speak up to fill the void. They may feel awkward enough not to do it again.

Praise Past Behaviour and Appeal to Better Instincts
'John, I have seen you be fair-minded and wasn't expecting you to make that kind of comment.'

Examine Assumptions/Statements Via Meta Models and Offer an Alternative Perspective
In Neuro Linguistic Programming (NLP), Meta Models allow you to obtain information from the speaker without assigning your own subjective meaning based on your experience. The following models let you gather high-quality information without being forced to make assumptions.

Deletions occur when you omit parts of an experience and make vague statements

Statement	Questions
I am scared of her.	Why specifically?
It's better not to say anything to her.	Better than what?
She is aggressive/controlling/moody/snappy.	How specifically/in what way?

Distortions take place when you modify the description of an experience. This often involves making assumptions by relating two experiences and/or jumping to conclusions

Statement	Questions
I know that she will not like/prefer/say/do. . .	How do you know that?
She is expecting and will be less committed.	How does her pregnancy make her less committed?
She is too loud for a girl.	According to whom? Who has defined the parameters of this behaviour?
She is yelling at me so she is bossy. She is doing poorly so she has low aptitude. She is quiet so she isn't confident.	How specifically does X mean Y?

Generalisations are statements in which you make general conclusions about an experience.

Statement	Questions
I can't do this, it's impossible!	What's stopping you?
I must/should/have to/need to do this.	Says who? What would happen if you did or didn't?
This happens all the time. They all do this.	Has there been a time when it did or didn't? Is there anyone who did or didn't?

As an additional resource, you may wish to revisit the questions listed under 'acknowledging your bias' earlier in the book.

Do the Labelling Exercise
You can do this exercise by yourself or with team members to explore the harmful impact of labelling using the following steps:

- What labels apply to you? Identify 10 and try to find at least four or five solid labels to work with.
- Determine whether each label is positive or negative.
- Where did the label come from (for example, media, TV, books or parents, peers, teachers, etc)? Be as specific as possible and name a specific person if you can.
- Do you agree with the label?
- Explore the benefits and drawbacks of each label. How does the label help you and how does it hinder or limit you?

- Are your labels getting in the way of achieving your goals?
- Which labels would you like to keep and which would you like to lose?
- Explore specific situations where the label is mentioned. Who are you with when you behave like the label? What could you do/how could you behave differently to make the label irrelevant or inappropriate?

Reframe

Reframing helps create a different way of looking at a situation, person, or relationship by changing its meaning. The technique considers that a person's point-of-view depends on the frame it is viewed in.

Example statement: 'She didn't get agreement at the meeting.'

Reframed: 'We have another opportunity to work on our arguments and persuade everyone individually.'

Example statement: 'She looks fed up.'

Reframed: 'It's time to take another approach—what could be more interesting for her?'

Share Personal Experiences

Demonstrating how sexism has negatively affected you or a woman close to you can help others understand its importance while reaffirming the experience of women in the organisation.

Make Use of Humour

I often recommend this strategy to diffuse a stressful situation at work. Sometimes a short, humorous observation or intervention can help you soften the call out. That does not suggest you aren't serious, but it's a way of letting off steam.

Use the Ouch Intervention

Good Guys recommend using the 'ouch intervention' when you are unsure what to say. You can simply say 'ouch,' which buys you an extra few seconds to coherently communicate what landed wrong with you. The same authors call this a #BroNo conversation. They even recommend a counter reinforcement if the perpetrator later shows some form of gender awareness using #GoBroGo.

Other Things to Look Out For
- The unnecessary mention of gender to divert a woman's attention from her professional prowess and remind her she is a woman before she steps into the spotlight. This intentionally shatters her confidence.
- Baseless comments about what women can and can't do.
- Outdated gender stereotypes.
- Sexist humour and gossip.
- Off topic comments and inappropriate questions.
- Pregnancy bias: listen for any comments about a woman's capability or performance while pregnant. This includes comments that marginalise and diminish the value of women.

CONFRONT DURING MEETINGS OR OTHER FORMAL GROUPS

Many women are regularly denounced at work through snide, belittling comments. They are often talked over and/or have their ideas stolen/co-opted during meetings. Allies help undermined women earn credit and recognition for their contributions. Colleagues can engage in *amplification*—a concept coined by the Obama White House offering women and a powerful strategy to address unconscious bias. Male allies who employ this strategy act as micro sponsors, giving credit where it's due, tactfully interjecting on behalf of their colleagues to include women and giving them an opportunity to weigh in.

Another tip: pay close attention to the seating arrangement. Men take up more space psychologically and physically while women tend to contort themselves into the smallest space and gravitate away from power positions at the head of the table. Check your spread, step aside and invite women to take power seats. . . perhaps even offer your own seat.

Call Out Interruptions Directly

- I would like her to finish what she is saying.
- Let's hear other viewpoints.
- Stop talking; it's time to listen.
- You just interrupted her.
- Every voice and every perspective needs to be heard.
- Let's give others a chance to speak.
- Let's hear your thoughts on this [XYZ]. This pull strategy aims to engage people who don't typically contribute.

Good Guys also recommends using a universal stop sign or time out sign as a hand gesture.

Other Ways to Discourage Interruptions

- Appoint a gatekeeper who tracks interruptions or idea usurpation.

- Establish meeting etiquette/no interruption policies.
- Throw the first *punch*. Resist temptation to talk. Create space. Ask a woman a specific question.
- Insist on her presence and participation and explain why it's essential.
- Highlight a participant's expertise, 'Anne has considerable experience in this area—let's hear what she thinks about this.'
- Strategically toss the ball (something trainers like myself do to engage all participants equally).
- Pull aside repeat offenders and talk to them about what they're doing.
- Encourage women to speak for themselves.

Handle 'Bropropriation'/Idea Hijacking

- Reinforce the idea/deflect the idea back to the originator, 'You forgot to give Ayesha a shout out.'
- Promote her idea/make it a discussion item, 'Today we will be discussing Sandra's idea.'
- Point out who did it/surface it earlier, 'Jasmin made the same point; let's give credit to her.'
- Redirect the credit, 'Pardon me, isn't this what Amna pointed out/shared earlier?'
- Recommend the idea to leadership with due credit. 'Today, in our weekly meeting Carol from the finance department offered this excellent suggestion. . .'

PREPARE FOR NEXT STEPS

If the bully remains undeterred, or you feel that there is serious risk in confrontation (such as being physically harmed or losing your job), then prepare for the next action. This could involve filing an internal complaint with the victim's manager who will typically give an opinion about the claim and discuss options. Encourage a victim to be prepared with her file of documented facts to defend her case. This file should include all bullying incidents and supporting materials. Keep it handy for future reference and make sure it details times, dates, and witnesses.

If the manager sides with a bully due to a personal friendship, or rationalises the mistreatment, you may need to involve HR/D&I representatives or other senior leaders in the company. If they are unable to help, the victim may need to pursue legal action or consider a change of environment. A toxic work culture that offers little chance of improvement will only adversely erode mental health over time.

If you successfully elevate the issue, don't let it end there. Continue efforts to drive long-term reform in your workplace; it will ultimately help create a more inclusive, collaborative culture.

CREATE A DOS AND DON'TS HANDBOOK

Support the creation, implementation and enforcement of a micro-aggression and harassment handbook. Its purpose is to protect employees from harm/retaliation. Elicit support from leadership and build awareness around dos and don'ts. Encourage consistency in publicly enforcing these rules—bullies often back down if they know they will be held accountable. The guide should detail inappropriate behaviours and include consequences for policy violations. It should also clearly highlight what to do if you see inappropriate behaviour—who to report it to and the steps leadership will take next to investigate the incident. You could also consider organising awareness sessions inviting senior leaders who are willing to share their own stories of reassessing behaviour, challenging limiting thought patterns and overcoming harmful biases - this would encourage others lower down the hierarchy to follow suit.

BUILD A SUPPORT NETWORK OF PEER ALLIES

Focus on the people who trust you and do not be discouraged by backlash for defending or speaking up for women in your circle. Establish a reliable set of supporters who can back your confrontation against the bullies. These peers or allies can also support you when you stand up for discrimination.

CONSIDER THE BIGGER PICTURE

There are no simple answers to why people behave inappropriately because human beings are quite complicated. We behave in a certain way to feel connected or to be heard, to minimise the sting of loss, or protect ourselves and the ones we love.

We do know that fear is a powerful trigger—the fear of failure, humiliation, loss of power, and/or rejection—as is low self-esteem. If you consider individuals struggling with drug or addiction issues, illness (their own or someone else's) and coping skills, you build a more complete picture of factors that can provoke difficult behaviour. Sometimes, of course, you'll run into a combination of factors. Some negative behaviours emerge as a result of various factors and influences - the absence or presence of which can trigger a reaction. Ask yourself if a lack of communication responsible for any behaviour or could it be the context of the situation?

Behaviours you thought you had influenced positively (or corrected altogether) can regress. If, as allies, we are content to only deal with surface issues versus digging down into deeper issues, we will fail to create a better workplace. We simply scrape the moss off the surface, only to have it to grow back later. Peeling an infraction back to its core takes patience and precision. Sometimes we avoid this because it can take time to uncover the real problem. We often find ourselves in too much of a hurry to address it properly. At other times, our emotions take over and we decide that we really don't want to go there because we will also have to face what is bothering us. If you don't stop to think about the big picture, you'll either miss the core problem or chase after too many problems at once.

SUMMARY

When a man suggests in a public forum that sexism has occurred, and thereby challenges the perpetrators, targets of sexism report greater self-confidence, as opposed to women who are often negatively evaluated when they personally report an issue.

Confront Privately

In choosing to respond, you could do so immediately or wait until you are in more control of your feelings. Here are few tips to bear in mind during any private confrontation.

Take Charge of Your Emotions

When you directly confront an individual, marshal your courage and temper your anxiety, especially if you are not in a leadership role that naturally commands respect and authority, or you are calling out someone senior to you.

Start Positive

Be polite and respectful. Don't aggravate the situation—remain calm and state why a behaviour or comment is offensive. Stick to exactly what has happened and don't exaggerate.

Be Direct

Use the first person point of view and say, 'I am [or XYZ] is feeling irritated/annoyed.' Don't distance yourself from your feelings with impersonal, third-person statements and generalisations such as, 'When people. . .' or 'It can be annoying when. . .' Use 'I' messages instead.

Share the Victim's Feelings of Threat and Fear

For example, 'She may be frightened of saying this to you because you might think she is being petty or you may reject her/fire her/hit her, but. . .' This will help you feel more in control of your feelings and may earn you some welcome and helpful reassurance.

Avoid Put Downs and Don't Invite Criticism or Retaliation
Don't say things such as, 'I know that she is a bit of a nag. . .' or 'She is over-sensitive.' By doing so you are sharing inflammatory ideas, validating the behaviour and unintentionally fanning the flames while confirming harmful gender stereotypes.

Confront Publicly
If you plan on confronting the aggressor publicly, these examples demonstrate how you can react and/or challenge in respectful ways.

Respond to Offensive Jokes
Some examples:

- I don't get it, can you explain?
- That wasn't funny at all!
- That's against our code of conduct.
- Did you really just say that?

Respond to Social/Physical Harassment
Statements such as, 'Get your hands off her' or 'Stay away from her' are firm, assertive and non-negotiable. Also, 'Is everything okay in here?' 'This behaviour is not acceptable.' 'We don't do that here!'

If you can't directly call out a violator for whatever reason, you can deploy a distraction or interruption strategy to start a conversation with the perpetrator and allow his potential target to safely exit the scene. If you are too embarrassed or shy to speak out, or if you don't feel comfortable doing so, ask someone else to step in. In any case, reach out and ask the victim later if she is okay and report it when it's safe to do so—it's never too late to act. Here are some other ways to handle the situation.

Ask a Reflective Question

Sometimes, when you repeat an offensive statement, others are forced to retreat or reflect on what they've said and how it might be received. For example, someone says, 'What I really want is for Susan to be less bossy' and you may respond by repeating their judgment word of choice. . .'Bossy?'

Pause

Simply stop talking. People often do not like silence and will invariably speak up to fill the void. They may feel awkward enough not to do it again.

Praise Past Behaviour and Appeal to Better Instincts

'John, I have seen you be fair-minded and wasn't expecting you to make that kind of comment.'

Examine Assumptions/Statements Via Meta Models and Offer an Alternative Perspective

In Neuro Linguistic Programming, Meta Models allow you to obtain information from the speaker without assigning your own subjective meaning based on your experience.

- **Deletions** occur when you omit parts of an experience and make vague statements.
- **Distortions** take place when you modify the description of

an experience. This often involves making assumptions by relating two experiences and/or jumping to conclusions.

- **Generalisations** happen when you make general conclusions about an experience.

Do the Labelling Exercise
You can do this exercise by yourself or with team members to explore the harmful impact of labelling.

Reframe
Reframing helps create a different way of looking at a situation, person, or relationship by changing its meaning. The technique considers that a person's point-of-view depends on the frame it is viewed in.

Make Use of Humour
I often recommend this strategy to diffuse a stressful situation at work. Sometimes a short, humorous observation or intervention can help you soften the call-out. That does not suggest you aren't serious, but it's a way of letting off steam.

Use the Ouch Intervention
Good Guys recommend using the 'ouch intervention' when you are unsure what to say. You can simply say 'ouch,' which buys you a few extra seconds to coherently communicate what landed wrong with you.

Other Things to Watch Out For
- The unnecessary mention of gender to divert a woman's attention from her professional prowess.
- Baseless comments about what women can't do.

- Outdated gender stereotypes.
- Sexist humour and gossip.
- Off topic comments and inappropriate questions.
- Pregnancy bias: listen for comments about a woman's capability or performance while pregnant. This includes comments that marginalise and diminish the value of women.

Confront During Meetings Or Other Formal Groups

Many women are regularly denounced at work through snide, belittling comments. They are often talked over and/or have their ideas stolen/co-opted during meetings. Allies help undermined women earn credit and recognition for their contributions.

Another tip is to pay close attention to the seating arrangement. Men take up more space psychologically and physically, while women tend to contort themselves into the smallest space and gravitate away from power positions at the head of the table.

Call Out Interruptions Directly
Examples:

- I would like her to finish what she is saying.
- Let's hear other viewpoints.
- Stop talking; it's time to listen.

Discourage Interruptions
Examples:

- Appoint a gatekeeper who tracks interruptions or idea usurpation.

- Establish meeting etiquette/no interruption policies.
- Throw the first *punch*. Resist temptation to talk. Create space. Ask a woman a specific question.

Handle 'Bropropriation'/Idea Hijacking
Examples:

- Reinforce the idea/deflect the idea back to the originator: 'You forgot to give Ayesha a shout out.'
- Promote her idea/make it a discussion item: 'Today we will be discussing Sandra's idea.'
- Point out who did it/surface it earlier: 'Jasmin made the same point; let's give credit to her.'

Prepare for Next Steps
If the bully remains undeterred, or you feel that there is serious risk in confrontation (such as being physically harmed or losing your job) then prepare for the next action. This could involve filing an internal complaint with the victim's manager. If you successfully elevate the issue, don't let it end there. Continue efforts to drive long term reform in your workplace; it will ultimately help create a more inclusive, collaborative culture.

Create a 'Dos and Don'ts' Handbook
Support the creation, implementation and enforcement of a micro-aggression and harassment handbook. Its purpose is to protect employees from harm/retaliation.

Elicit support from leadership and build awareness around dos and don'ts. Encourage consistency in publicly enforcing these rules—bullies often back down if they know they will be held accountable.

Build a Support Network of Peer Allies

Focus on the people who trust you and do not be discouraged by backlash for defending or speaking up for women in your circle. Establish a reliable set of supporters who can back your confrontation against the bullies.

Consider the Bigger Picture

Behaviours you thought you had influenced positively (or corrected altogether) can regress. If, as allies, we are content to only deal with surface issues versus digging down into deeper issues, we will fail to create a better workplace.

SECTION 3

CHALLENGE THE ORGANISATIONAL CULTURE

'Each time a man stands up for an ideal, or acts to improve the lot
of others, or strikes out against injustice,
he sends forth a tiny ripple of hope.'
-Robert F Kennedy-

We often believe that our career trajectories are the result of our individual strengths and accomplishments, not the composition of the organisation. However, it is the business culture—a culture that penalises women who work from home with sick children; a culture that makes balancing work and family nearly impossible for women—and the criteria for success that typically shape a woman's career path. Women regularly experience gender bias, and the processes by which they are evaluated are gendered too. What's more, the culture and system keep the role of a career professional and mother mutually exclusive, when in reality they are not.

In our *Her Allies* panel discussion, participants noted the importance of changing hearts and minds before you try to change policy. The group observed that it is relatively easy to write and create a policy—a flexible work policy, for example, supports women and men as they juggle personal and professional responsibilities. However, it is much harder to advocate for an organisation to implement that policy. If an organisation's culture fails to reward or recognise those who work part- or flex-time, and this working arrangement is considered a barrier to progression, then this policy will be perceived as a superficial 'quick fix.' Policies alone will not transform an organisation's culture; the company must first be receptive to change and united in driving that change. Remember, the individuals within the organisation have the power to set the tone for the organisation.

So far, you have called yourself out for any problematic behaviour that you may have unintentionally engaged in and summoned courage to call out others (thank you for being a true ally!). You are now ready to tackle the more significant organisational issues and move from being an ally to a change agent who can establish accountability and transparency, and use your position to slowly but steadily transform the organisation's culture. The language is still direct and action-oriented, but from here onwards, the discussion is more about 'potential impact.' Even if you are not a senior HR or D&I leader, you still have the power to shift perceptions and priorities by applying your knowledge and focus to critical issues. After all, as novelist Alice Walker points out, 'The most common way people give up their power is by thinking they don't have any.' Let's look at some of the overarching policies you can influence just by getting involved.

PERFORM A CULTURE AUDIT

An organisation's culture has a strong influence on whether men acknowledge the existence of gender disparities. Many organisations position their structure as meritocratic, supported by inclusive human resource policies and practices that are invulnerable to bias. But this meritocracy myth often masks bias and gender inequalities because there is no commitment to checks and balances that help alleviate these issues. The pandemic and Black Lives Matter movement have exposed many ubiquitous loopholes in the system that continue to erode marginalised communities and impede true progress. Have a good look around and check if your culture is unconsciously encouraging bias. Are employees penalised for taking time off but not for inciting hateful speech? Is family leave difficult to secure but misplaced humour and micro-aggressions targeting marginalised groups are a dime a dozen? Are employees working late and contacted outside of office hours? Is working culture rife with locker room talk? Does the work ambience seem divisive—are employees always on the edge, pitted against each other? If the answer is yes to any of the above, then it's time for a change.

A robust Equality, Diversity and Inclusion (EDI) plan is now more important than ever. Every company is unique, hence it is crucial to identify the context in which any D&I framework operates, including the regulatory or legal environment as well as the size, structure and culture of that organisation. While the strategic budget is proportionate to an organisation's size and resources, the good news is many companies can implement several changes at zero or minimum cost. Most of the impactful changes begin with one simple step: creating awareness. And that's where you, as an ally, can add value to ensure that these awareness efforts are integrated into the organisation's culture and day-to-day activities.

From recruitment to talent management, appraisal to compensation, management needs to revisit all organisational policies and systems to check for overt and covert bias that is weighted against women and impacts their opportunities for career progression. A revamp should also include re-allocating existing staff or resources, creating new policies and procedures as needed, hiring necessary staff and imparting fresh skills and training aligned with equality regulations. Gender and inclusion initiatives must be connected with leadership development and training. Staff members should be trained on conscious and unconscious bias, and every decision should be informed by a structured due diligence process.

What's more, a company should implement steps to develop female talent. The latter need access to informal networks, influential mentors and stretch assignments. Research proves that diversity leads to richer, more productive, more sustainable decisions. Yet, women comprise just five percent of Fortune 500 CEOS, and they were also under-represented in Covid-19 global health decision-making and leadership bodies. This is symptomatic of our wider society, where women continue to be under-represented in leadership roles and boardrooms. As an ally, you can push for change by mentoring and sponsoring women in your circle and ensuring that they are included in key decisions and opportunities. But while you do that, remember that tokenism exacerbates gender bias and fosters resentment, as it suggests that women in leadership positions did not rightfully earn their positions. Avoid tokenism at all costs. Sometimes, during recruitment, female candidates may be concerned with tokenism screening, so you can assure them that the process has been fair and anonymous.

As a team leader or manager, you need to hold managers accountable for diversity decisions while discouraging stereotypes that influence those decisions. Organisations can also conduct an Effective Pay-Equity Audit and share results with employees to build trust and transparency. Clear policies and awareness of those policies help reduce the likelihood of sexism and other prejudices. Soliciting feedback is a critical part of this development process so that management can identify and address any subtle filters. Anonymous surveys and feedback can help develop a solid, evidence-based understanding of the underlying causes of any diversity and inclusion gaps. As an ally, you can play an active role in supporting a comprehensive assessment by soliciting feedback from female colleagues through interviews, surveys and brainstorm sessions. Post-pandemic, there may be unique challenges impacting female colleagues that an organisation had not anticipated, so keep those in mind. For a more sophisticated implementation, be prepared to hire experts and specialised consultants who can move beyond the basic framework.

To effectively counter harassment and other forms of provocations, your business must actively deploy mitigation, not just containment, strategies. You and your organisation will also need to develop, monitor/track and review the progress on a regular basis. Typically, comprehensive annual reviews are adequate, but in the current climate, a semi-annual evaluation is warranted. Any knowledge or skill gap identified in the review should be addressed soon after. Finally, make sure to set and communicate expectations and measurable results. Employees are often not invested until they know what's in it for them.

Author Simon Sinek encourages finding your *why* to discover your life's purpose—and finding fulfilment through purpose—which in turn helps you prioritise your goals. If your *why* relates to your inclusion efforts, then you will be that much more committed to allyship. We identified this *why* at the beginning of Chapter One. But Julie Kratz, founder of Pivot Point, further recommends crafting a unified and shared purpose to support your company's EDI plan. If you establish a plan dashboard, as Kratz suggests, then you will also be able to link employee performance to the EDI plan to ensure commitment. Ensure Key Performance Indicators (KPIs or metrics) are in place and that leadership regularly evaluates those against program goals. As an ally, you can help check for bias and keep a vigilant eye on deviations from established benchmarks.

INVEST IN WOMEN-FOCUSED EMPLOYEE RESOURCE GROUPS AND NETWORKS

Many organisations do not invest sufficient time and money in staff networks that can be crucial in a crisis or even otherwise. They also offer a good starting point for discussing gender specific issues or issues related to other marginalised groups.

Employees feel more secure when they are part of affinity groups with members who share the same fears and challenges. Gender and race networks can play a huge role in advocating for marginalised groups. Michelle Bogan, Founder and CEO of Equity at Work, suggests women need to see action across participation, resources and policy decisions; companies must do right by women, which includes consistently taking a stand on the day-to-day micro-aggressions and bigger-deal issues. She notes, 'We made a ton of progress working from the ground up, but there were limits to how far we could go without the partnership of male colleagues and buy-in from leadership, all the way to the most senior level.' As an ally, it's important for you to demonstrate how much you value women and their contributions. As an advocate, you are not just standing up for them, you are joining them in their fight for equality, so actively participating in these sessions (should men be invited) sends a powerful message of solidarity.

IMPROVE PARENTAL LEAVE BENEFITS

Managing home responsibilities has traditionally been a woman's job, thus there is an expectation that career women will flex their schedule and realign commitments because that is what society dictates. Introducing non-transferable rights that enable both parents to take leave in the first year of their child's birth is an important gender equality measure that has also improved father-child relationships.

In Sweden, for example, state policies encourage men to take parental leave and be part of their children's first months. Before the creation of 'Daddy Days,' fewer than 20 percent of Swedish men took any parental leave at all. Today, more than 90 percent take advantage of this dedicated family time. Finland's government also announced plans to give all parents the same parental leave in an effort that encourages fathers to spend more time with their children. Men need to demand parental leave, policies need to encourage and support it, and the culture of our organisations needs to shift so that men taking leave is the new norm—because only when men share housework and childcare will women be able to balance work and family and truly have it all. This is, as it seems to me, the promise of gender mainstreaming.

In 2009, the UK granted paternity leave for the first time. Unfortunately, the data indicates men are not taking advantage of the new policy because employers do not pay paternity leave at a rate that compensates men for the loss of their (generally) higher salary. Thus, the financial loss is a practical consideration that can often outweigh the desire for family time off, especially for a new father who often bears responsibility as the 'breadwinner.'

We also need to accommodate mothers who would rather take more time off. They should not feel pressure to return to work to avoid being penalised. The pandemic has disproportionately shifted the burden of home chores back onto women, leaving them fatigued and anxious. That burden is especially cumbersome for single parents who cannot turn to outside help during quarantine or lockdown. Moreover, women are also more likely to be single parents than men are. A 2020 report by TrustRadius revealed that women in tech are more likely to be laid-off or furloughed than men, and nearly one and a half times as likely to feel a greater childcare burden due to Covid-19. Fourteen percent of women are considering quitting their jobs because of family demands the pandemic created. Deciding to leave the workforce can have long term financial ramifications for women who are already lagging behind in terms of pay, pension and health insurance.

As an ally, you can set an example by taking parental leave yourself and championing others who do. In earlier chapters, I provide tips on how to lead with empathy and focus on the mental and physical wellbeing of employees—those efforts can go a long way toward influencing an individual's decision to take time off or work through critical family milestones. Mentoring and sponsoring women can also help them make optimal decisions for their personal situations.

PROVIDE WORK FLEXIBILITY

Flexible benefits usually include reduced hours, job sharing, work from home options, a compressed work week, or a leave of absence with leeway in assignment completion. Given the dramatic, fast-paced global changes, it is important to keep reassessing current priorities while projecting sensitivity and empathy in all communications. Covid-19 has provided an opportunity for companies to adopt gender-inclusive and family-friendly workplace policies and practices, including flexible work arrangements that can disrupt gender stereotypes, change traditional narratives, and encourage more balanced share of care and family responsibilities.

Within the last year, we have experienced a dramatic shift

towards telecommuting and a work from home revolution—the pandemic is an inflection point dictating the future of work. Organisations now recognise the value of telecommuting, particularly when the alternative is not working at all. Many established businesses have already realised financial savings from the telecommuting trend. Sun Microsystems identified US$68 million a year in real estate savings, while Dow Chemical and Nortel have saved more than 30 percent on non-real estate costs. Companies now know it is possible to replace off-site events with video conferences, and that travel reduction continues to positively impact our planet. Moving forward, women and young mothers, in particular, can continue benefiting from this trend even after normalcy resumes. An employee physically working within an office does not necessarily guarantee improved performance or productivity. Flexible work hours, work from home opportunities, job sharing, and part-time jobs (when appropriate) can ensure companies retain talented mothers during their child-rearing years.

As an ally and leader, you can actively push for these policy adjustments, not just for your own team but on an organisational level. The Women's Equalities Committee UK recommends that the British Government amend the Flexible Working Regulations 2014 to remove the 26-weeks' service threshold for employees to request flexible working arrangements. It is also recommended the GEO and EHRC explore the feasibility of reporting on parental leave policies in addition to gender gaps in furlough and redundancies for 2020/21 to supplement the information on pay and bonuses.

SUPPORT ON-SITE CHILDCARE

Those organisations that do plan to return to physical workspaces could consider incorporating on-site childcare facilities wherever possible keeping social distancing requirements in mind. This might not be easy to implement, but many companies have successfully done so already. Moreover, studies indicate that employee performance is higher and absenteeism lower among employees using on-site versus offsite childcare. On-site crèche facilities offer convenience and peace of mind. Employees feel valued and work harder to exceed expectations. In addition, on-site childcare also helps reduce tardiness and stress while alleviating separation anxiety. Plus, children in the workplace can add much-needed energy and cheer, and help employees be more mindful of aggressive, disruptive conflicts.

IMPROVE WORK-LIFE BALANCE FOR MEN AND WOMEN

The prevalence of long working hours has had a negative impact on women's employment. Policies in this regard tend to favour men over women and thus reinforce gender stereotypes while magnifying differences between paid and unpaid work. The ideal work-life balance is more elusive for women because we are more likely to manage household and family care responsibilities.

While research indicates that the gender pay gap is narrowing for young workers, it is widening among working mothers, as they are effectively suffering a pay penalty for taking time off or working fewer hours than men. Technology that facilitates answering emails at all hours in the evening puts working mothers at a disadvantage, as they already bear the disproportionate burden of domestic responsibilities. Organisations need to stop valuing presenteeism and on-call availability to level the playing field for mothers.

OFFER FREE UNIVERSAL CHILDCARE

One of the most significant hurdles that prevents women from reaching the top of their career is the lack of affordable childcare support. As I highlighted in *Her Way To The Top*, in the UK childcare is very expensive, which makes most British mothers opt to stay at home even though they would like to work after giving birth. A report by OECD highlights how, as a proportion of household income, the UK has the most expensive childcare in the world. In Sweden, for instance, where childcare is heavily subsidised, it costs parents up to three percent of household income, instead of the UK's average of about 35 percent. Author and Founder of Charity, Pregnant Then Screwed, says that childcare should be considered an essential infrastructure and not just a 'soft option.' As an ally, you can encourage your organisation to provide benefits that involve paying for child and elderly care.

The pandemic has forced people to pay attention to this overlooked benefit. According to a Trade Union Congress survey, two in every five working mothers with children under the age of 10 in the UK are struggling to find childcare, as breakfast and after-school clubs remain shut, and care amongst friends and family remains limited.

I was recently mentoring a woman who had moved closer to her mother to help care for her during the pandemic. The move negatively impacted her career opportunities. This is a women's issue—not just an issue for working mothers.

'Lack of childcare access risks turning the clock back on decades of labour market progress,' warns Frances O'Grady, General Secretary of the Trades Union Congress. And CEO of Working Families, Jane van Zyl, notes parents were expected to return to work in a similar way to pre-Covid times but without vital childcare infrastructure, 'Caring responsibilities have been absent from the government's economic recovery plans, and they now need to be centre stage.'

Caroline Nokes, chair of the Women and Equalities Select Committee, recognises the government has failed to heed months of warnings about the *real crisis* looming. She says, 'We want women to come out of this pandemic in as good an employment position as men, and without some proactive policy to bring that about, it will simply not happen.'

The government needs to allocate a budget to childcare. According to the Women's Budget Group, investing two percent of the GDP in the care industry would generate up to one and a half million jobs in the UK, compared to US$750,000 for an equivalent investment in construction. A report by the same group also revealed that up to 95 percent of the cost of free universal pre-school childcare could be recouped from the increase in employment and job creation, and reduced benefits. Moreover, high-quality, early-years education is also linked to better life chances for children.

The Women's Equalities Committee recommends that 'the Government publish, by June 2021, an early year's strategy which sets out how childcare provision can best support not only working parents, but also those who are job-seeking and re-training. The review must also consider the feasibility of extending eligibility for free childcare provision for children under the age of three years.'

SUPPORT INCLUSIVE NETWORKING OPPORTUNITIES

Building a network of 'the right' people can help women move up the corporate ladder. The best career opportunities often arise from interactions outside the office, but women tend to miss out on these interactions. As an ally you can work to arrange social interaction opportunities that women and men can attend together such as 'lunch and learn' sessions, book clubs, and podcast discussions. You can even invite partners or whole families if some women feel uncomfortable attending on their own. This was quite common when I worked in Pakistan. Perhaps it was a cultural thing and every person has their own likes and preferences, but I always welcomed invitations to events outside of work, especially those scheduled after work hours when my family was invited too. I also recommend that you let women choose the venue, but don't pressure them to attend. Some may have care responsibilities at home, but extending the invitation is what matters most, as well as ensuring that the nature of these outings is inclusive to all.

STRUCTURE DIVERSE EVENTS

Many organisations overlook the value of diverse events. Too often, they are skewed. It's likely that you have organised, or at least attended, a company event in the past. As an ally, you can play a role in creating diverse events that represent all genders and various ethnicities. All-male panels and male keynote speakers continue to be the rule rather than the exception. In some cases, men become the authorities on women in business and academia, without a career woman or female professor in sight! To ensure inclusive events, consider creating a diverse planning committee composed of diverse voices. Strictly discourage 'manels' with all-male panel participants. If you are asked to be part of a homogenous panel, suggest others who can help create a more diverse pool. Ideally, there is an event Code of Conduct that all participants must adhere to; anyone who violates the code will be asked to leave. Before accepting a speaking engagement or registering for an event, Karen

Catlin recommends requesting this Code of Conduct. Ensure events are accessible for all, offer changing rooms for parents (if it's an event with children) include provisions for prayer rooms, etc. Wherever possible, include accessibility information about transportation, parking, seating arrangement and personal space, and the availability of interpreting services or assistive listening devices.

Presentation and marketing materials need to be similarly diverse, as do speaker slides and the event playlist!

Speakers can be provided with accessibility notes, it will also be useful to remind the speakers to speak clearly (ideally facing forward without covering their mouth), avoid using acronyms and colloquialisms and exercise discretion when making use of different pronouns.

Avoid offensive or sexualised images in promotional materials. Make sure there are non-alcoholic options along with an assortment of food that caters to all types of dietary requirements including vegetarian, vegan/halal/kosher and gluten-free options. Most importantly, ensure that all food/consumables are properly labelled and where possible, ingredients and allergens listed. I cannot believe how many D&I events I have attended that left me guessing the menu and peeling apart sandwiches to check if I was eating tuna or chicken! It is recommended to reach out to attendees both during and after the event to elicit feedback, confirm if they were comfortable, informed, and able to fully participate and use that information to inform future events.

BE TRANSPARENT ABOUT THE PAY GAP

Transparency means being open about processes, policies and decision-making criteria. Employees are clear on what is involved and trust that managers will make objective, evidence-based decisions because the system is structured to hold them accountable. Introducing transparency to promotion, pay and reward processes can also reduce pay inequalities.

A new culture of transparency will challenge companies to investigate the gender and ethnicity pay gap. One small but meaningful step: HR professionals should stop asking candidates for compensation history and instead offer a salary bracket or range for an open position. Women are less likely to negotiate their pay. This may be because they aren't sure what a reasonable offer is. By revealing salary range, women are empowered to negotiate. Many allies share their salaries with female colleagues to ensure they aren't short-changed by their gender, especially if they have the same experience and potential.

Buffer, a social media management company, shares salary details for each staff member and provides a salary calculator that lets candidates quickly calculate what they could earn across roles if they join the company. While this level of transparency may not be feasible for every organisation, introducing salary brackets for each position will help eliminate bias. The report, *Unequal Impact? Coronavirus and the Gendered Economic Impact*, recommends that gender pay gap reporting be urgently reinstated.

SUPPORT IMPARTIAL HIRING PRACTICES

If you are leading a team, then you have likely been involved in an organisation's recruitment process. As an ally and leader, you are in a position to drive change.

The recruitment process itself, including the language, web page and job description, should be gender neutral. The goal is to attract diverse talent so make sure you showcase diverse employees within your materials; candidates are more likely to apply if they believe your company values diverse perspectives. Post open jobs across a variety of outlets and reward employees for diverse referrals that expand your talent pool.

Attract qualified female candidates through inclusive messaging that speaks to; corporate culture and broader Corporate Social Responsibility (CSR) initiatives that unite employees with social causes.

As you identify your shortlist of qualified candidates, make sure to include more than one woman so the 'we don't have enough female candidates' excuse does not apply. Moreover, shortlists with only one woman diminishes the chance of a woman being selected.

Rather than relying on interviews only, you can ask candidates to perform skills-based assessments related to the role they are applying for. Use their performance on those tasks to assess their suitability for the role. Standardise the tasks and scoring metrics to ensure equitable evaluations across candidates.

Establishing objective criteria for reviewing resumés can help reduce bias, as does using structured interviews for recruitment and promotions. There are benefits and drawbacks to structured versus unstructured interviews, but know that unstructured ones are more likely to permit unfair bias to creep in and influence decision-making. The ideal structured interview asks exactly the same questions of all candidates in a predetermined order and format then evaluates responses using pre-specified, standardised criteria. This ensures comparable responses and reduces the impact of unconscious bias.

In the beginning of the process, interviewers should have a checklist describing biases and actionable advice to mitigate them.

Watch out for statements such as:

- Not sure candidate X is a good fit/cultural fit.
- She looks like a busy mum. (Inferring a candidate's family obligations.)
- She's not likeable.
- Smart women are sexy.
- She could use some make-up.
- Is she single?

In my role as a Senior Advisory Team Leader, I interviewed candidates for the BENU L.E.A.D.S women's leadership program. The interview notes advised interviewers to keep the 'IF-THEN' concept in mind—a framework that I found useful. 'IF I find myself immediately jumping to conclusions about a person, THEN, I am going to give special focus to listening more intently to find the unique perspective this person offers versus shutting her down.'

According to the Neuro Leadership Institute, there are more than 150 existing biases which they have organised into five broad categories. These five biases comprise the SEEDS Model® which help us understand and mitigate our own bias during decision making in the interview process:

1. **Similarity Bias**: We prefer what is like us over what is different.
2. **Expedience Bias**: We prefer to act quickly rather than take time.
3. **Experience Bias**: We take our perception to be the objective truth.
4. **Distance Bias**: We prefer what's closer over what's farther away.
5. **Safety Bias**: We protect against loss more than we seek out gain.

Other common biases to be aware of:

- **In-Group Bias**: Perceiving those who are similar in a more positive way.
- **Halo Effect**: The tendency to believe only good about someone because they are likeable. Letting someone's positive qualities in one area influence the overall perception of that person.
- **Confirmation Bias**: The tendency to seek information that confirms pre-existing beliefs or assumptions, or conversely to discount information that is incongruent with one's assumptions.
- **Group Think**: The tendency to try and fit into a particular group by mimicking their behaviour or holding back on sharing thoughts and opinions out of fear of potential exclusion.
- **Anchoring Bias**: The tendency to rely heavily upon the first piece of information available rather than seeking out and fully evaluating multiple sources of information for optimal decision-making.

Many organisations claim that diversity quotas force them to lower their bar even though in reality the hiring process typically favours a particular gender. Focus on understanding a candidate's journey—that may be more valuable to the team than years of experience. Karen Catlin recommends asking yourself if the 'nice to have column' is necessary and eliminating whatever content isn't critical to the evaluation. If you have to choose between two equally qualified team members, Karen suggests making an offer to the candidate who will diversify your team. Finally, it is helpful to record ongoing anonymous feedback on the recruitment process to identify any loopholes and incorporate suggestions accordingly. To that point, exit interviews are equally important to gauge the underlying reasons for employee departures. Open-ended questions and probing techniques, as noted earlier, can offer valuable insight into workplace culture.

GIVE UNBIASED APPRAISALS

As highlighted earlier, women often get short-changed in reviews and miss out on critical talent assessment discussions. Behavioural Economist Dr. Paola Cecchi-Dimeglio discovered that women receive more subjective annual reviews than objectives ones. She notes, 'Because annual evaluations *are* often subjective, that opens the door to gender bias ('Tom is more comfortable and independent than Carolyn in handling the client's concerns') and confirmation bias ('I knew she'd struggle with that project'), among other things.'

She also singles out a review that included a glaring difference in words used to describe similar situations, 'Heidi seems to shrink when she's around others, and especially around clients. She needs to be more self-confident,' versus 'Jim needs to develop his natural ability to work with people.'

In another pair of reviews, the reviewer highlighted the woman's *analysis paralysis*, while the same behaviour in a male colleague was described as, *careful thoughtfulness*.

Paola recommends using more objective criteria, involving a broader group of reviewers, and adjusting the frequency of reviews to remove subjective biases that creep in. Associate Professor Lauren Riviera proposes experimenting with metrics and evaluation tools to discover new ways to *move the needle*. This may not eliminate deeply ingrained gender stereotypes but in sociologist Joan William's words, they might *interrupt* their effect on ratings and begin to bridge career gender gaps. As an ally, you play a crucial role in removing bias when you or your team evaluate a woman's performance. That is also an opportunity to ensure promotions are not skewed in favour of dominant groups.

CATER TO EXPECTANT MOTHERS AND NEW MOTHERS

Even if your company has few women employees, deliberate on incorporating a full range of policies to support pregnant women, including different types of leaves, parental leaves, lactation rooms and onsite mother rooms. Ignoring an employee's personal needs and situation sabotages productivity. If there are pregnant women in your team, discuss their career plan with them and offer flexible options. Make sure that paid family leave does not negatively impact career advancement.

Some enlightened governments extend leave for unfortunate circumstances surrounding a pregnancy or birth. In Pakistan, the local Government in Sindh province offers working mothers one week maternity leave in case of a miscarriage, four weeks for a stillborn birth and 16 weeks in case of a premature delivery Other countries that offer such extended leaves include India, Mauritius, Philippines, Indonesia and Taiwan. New Zealand's parliament made news in early 2021 by unanimously passing legislation that would entitle mothers and their partners to bereavement leave following a pregnancy loss or still birth. The Bereavement Leave for Miscarriage Bill will give a couple three paid days off work to grieve and recover from a pregnancy loss. 'The Bill will give women and their partners' time to come to terms with their loss without having to tap into sick leave. Because their grief is not a sickness, it is a loss,' said the Bill's sponsor, Ginny Andersen, a member of the Labour Party led by Prime

Minister Jacinda Ardern. These are difficult times for parents, so governments or organisations recognising this is a welcome change.

The Women's and Equality Committee, in a report published in February 2020, recommends introducing legislation to extend redundancy protection to pregnant women and new mothers. The report also urges that government to publish a cross-departmental strategy, following consultation with stakeholders, for dealing with pregnancy and maternity discrimination.

EXTEND FLEXIBILITY TO EVERYONE

On that note, pregnant or working mothers are not the only ones who need attention—everyone including non-binary people should have the opportunity to thrive and have their needs respected. Single and childless workers require policies that protect their needs too. These groups may have other care responsibilities or difficult situations that flexibility and support can help resolve. After her husband passed way, Sheryl Sandberg, Chief Operating Officer of Facebook, realised the need for bereavement leave and introduced this policy at the company.

During the pandemic, many people moved closer to elderly parents to support and nurture them. When I resumed work following my wedding leave, my HR Director asked if I needed to leave early during the first few weeks and ensured there were no late sittings. I appreciated my manager's focus on my needs and personal situation—his concern made me feel valued and respected. As an ally, keeping an eye out for individuals that may need flexibility owing to their unique situations and subsequently making adjustments to accommodate them, can go a long way in making these employees feel appreciated.

INVOLVE KEY STAKEHOLDERS AND INVEST IN WOMEN-FOCUSED INITIATIVES

Finally, your actions around diversity will impact communities surrounding you. Extend your goals and vision to your suppliers and customers, share your agenda with key stakeholders so they are inspired to follow suit. Share the steps you are taking to promote diversity on your end.

If you can afford to, provide guidance to the local, national or global communities that you work with to build trust and long-term relationships. Also, proudly champion the culture of zero tolerance for bias and harassment. A strong policy will put your females colleagues at ease and reassure them that they do not have to do business with any client who makes them feel uncomfortable.

As an ally, you can also encourage your organisation to support employers and trade unions that represent female-dominated labour market sectors. During Covid-19, women are one of the most negatively impacted social groups. To address this, UN Women recommends a multi-stakeholder engagement, which ensures a gender-sensitive response to the pandemic guided by female politicians, key influencers and decision makers. The latter demands that women's voices and interests are reflected in the decision-making processes and women are represented on task forces and response teams.

If you are in a position to influence organisational spending on CSR projects, encourage leadership to consider redirecting women-owned business/micro-business budgets to 'gender lens investing'—investing in products and services that benefit and empower women socially and economically, including promoting education as a catalyst for female leadership. Your organisation can also make a difference by sponsoring women's organisations and shelters.

There is a plethora of organisations working tirelessly to defend women's rights. Our female predecessors fought to secure the basic rights we enjoy today, but in many parts of the world, women are still abused, traded, mutilated, and deprived of education. Honour killings, child brides, and acid attacks remain a sad reality for thousands of our global sisters. These women need your support.

Global women's marches highlight what we can achieve when we organise and mobilise. When you are part of/in touch with an organisation working to support women, you have a proper platform to champion issues important to you and connect with like-minded individuals.

STAY THE COURSE

It is important to recognise what stage your organisation is at in terms of gender equality and male allyship. The *Men as Allies: Engaging Men to Advance Women in the Workplace* report suggests that if your employees are not ready for significant changes, adjust your strategy or tempo, and try to meet your male employees 'where they are.' It recommends striking a balance between acknowledging the feelings of men who are reluctant to step up, while professionally and respectfully challenging resistant attitudes.

Effectively managing change and introducing new policy involves communication, culture pacing, accountability and success metrics. Poorly planned change that is implemented too quickly wastes resources, promotes confusion and often has financial repercussions. It also lowers morale and compromises opportunities across the organisation.

The process of change can progress from acceptance to denial followed by confusion and ultimately, renewal. Everett M. Rogers who is best known for developing the *diffusion of innovations theory*, believed that people's reactions fall into the following categories:

- Innovators
- Early Adopters
- Early Majority
- Late Majority
- Late Adopters
- Diehards

The Innovators try things first, followed by the Early Adopters. These are people you need to get on board first. Focus your efforts on them, not the Diehards. Some people will never change and you cannot spend your own time trying to convert them. They become casualties of change.

When five percent of people in a group adopt a change, the change is embedded. When 20 percent adopt it, the change is unstoppable. Get the Innovators and Early Adopters on board and you assure the success of your change.

The following coaching models may have value for you as a change agent.

The Grow Model

G: Goals	R: Reality
1. What would you like to work on?	1. What actions have you taken so far?
2. What would you like to achieve? (a first step/strategy/solution)?	2. What actions will move your closer to the goals
3. When are you going to do to achieve it?	3. What is getting in the way?
4. What are the personal benefits/advantages for achieving this goal?	4. What are you more clear about; direction or interest?
5. Who else will benefit and in what way?	5. Why do you believe you aren't any clearer?
6. What will it be like if you achieve your goal?	6. What is standing between you and that clarity
7. How will you know if you've got it?	
8. What would it look/feel/sound like?	

O: Options	W: Will
1. What different options and possibilities do you already have to achieve your goal? 2. What options can you create? 3. What else could you do? 4. What has/ hasn't worked? 5. What are the key advantages and disadvantages of each option?	1. Which options have you chosen to act on? 2. When and what action will you take? And after that? 3. What would you pursue if you knew you couldn't fail? 4.What would you do in this situation if you knew that no one would judge you? 5. What is your gut telling you to do? 6. What is the simplest step that you can take in the right direction? 7. What action would you take if you trusted yourself more? 8. What action that takes one hour or less to complete could move you in the direction of achieving your goals?

The Benefit/Consequence Matrix

This matrix lists the benefits and consequences of changing versus benefits and consequences of not changing for a more informed choice.

Engaging Men in Gender Initiatives: What Change Agents Need to Know highlights the importance and value of organising male-only dialogues. Consider arranging open and candid conversations amongst men, where men can express their point of view freely and listen to other points of view. These sessions can help them reconsider their stance otherwise you risk securing tacit agreement— more of a lip-service—where men give consent begrudgingly without any real understanding of barriers to equality and how to dismantle them. In the exclusive company of other men, men are in a 'safe space" and thus are more likely to share their perspective without fear of blame or accusation. Otherwise anxieties can prevent men from partnering with women to advance gender equality issues and participate in related discussions.

You may leverage repetition and reinforcement respectfully to keep things on track. Conversations are easily derailed, especially if participants get emotional, or someone is trying to steer the conversation away from your primary message. Do not be afraid to restate your purpose during an interaction. Continuously hold discussions and make sure information is easy to understand and not overwhelming. Use short videos or presentation polls, gamification and other engagement tools to keep others involved.

For nearly a decade, The Volvo Group has been working to engage men in the advancement of women through its *Walk the Talk* program. Implemented in 1998, the program seeks to promote greater awareness and understanding of gender and leadership issues and their impact on Volvo's business development, managers, and the organisation as a whole. One practice that has helped support this initiative is introducing reverse mentors. These partnerships enable each male participant to select a female mentor trained on leadership and gender issues to follow her mentee's progress throughout the program. Research indicates that men who had female mentors were more aware of gender bias than men who only had male mentors. Findings suggest respected women colleagues can play an important role in educating men about gender bias by offering support and challenging men to think more critically about gender relations in the workplace. Hence, you may also want to encourage your company to incorporate reverse mentoring or cross-gender mentoring.

Finally, if a man feels like everyone else at work is supporting women, then he is more likely to support women as well. As they say—the proof is in the pudding! Influential managers and male allies can play a critical role here. Share examples of how best-in-class companies and "courageous male role models" (as Volvo calls them) are taking action to address gender equality then encourage others to join the alliance.

SUMMARY

Perform a Culture Audit

Have a good look around and check if your culture is unconsciously encouraging bias. From recruitment to talent management, appraisal to compensation, management needs to revisit all organisational policies and systems to check for overt and covert bias that is weighted against women and impacts their opportunities for career progression. A revamp should also include re-allocating existing staff or resources, creating new policies and procedures as needed, hiring necessary staff and imparting fresh skills and training aligned with equality regulations.

Invest in Women-Focused Employee Resource Groups and Networks

Many organisations do not invest sufficient time and money in staff networks that can be crucial in a crisis and help build valuable connections between employees. They also offer a good starting point for discussing gender-specific issues or issues related to other marginalised groups.

Improve Parental Leave Benefits

Managing home responsibilities has traditionally been a woman's job, thus there is an expectation that career women will flex their schedule and realign commitments because that is what society dictates. Introducing non-transferable rights that enable both parents to take leave in the first year of their child's birth is an important gender equality measure that also improves father-child relationships.

Provide Work Flexibility

Flexible benefits usually include reduced hours, job sharing, work from home options, a compressed work week, or a leave of absence with leeway in assignment completion. Given the dramatic, fast-paced global changes, it is important to keep reassessing current priorities while projecting sensitivity and empathy in all communications. Covid-19 has granted companies an opportunity to adopt gender-inclusive and family-friendly workplace policies and practices.

Support On-Site Childcare
Those organisations that do plan to return to physical workspaces could consider incorporating on-site childcare facilities wherever possible, keeping social distancing requirements in mind.

Improve Work-Life Balance for Men and Women
Technology that facilitates answering emails at all hours of the evening puts working mothers at a disadvantage, as they already bear the disproportionate burden of domestic responsibilities. Organisations need to stop valuing presenteeism and on-call availability to level the playing field for mothers.

Offer Free Universal Childcare
One of the most significant hurdles that prevents women from reaching the top of their career is the lack of affordable childcare support. As an ally, you can encourage your organisation to provide benefits that involve paying for child and elderly care.

Support Inclusive Networking Opportunities

Building a network of 'the right' people can help women move up the corporate ladder. The best career opportunities often arise from interactions outside the office, but women tend to miss out on these connections. Work to arrange social interaction opportunities that everyone can attend together, such as 'lunch and learn' sessions, book clubs and podcast discussions.

Structure Diverse Events
Many organisations overlook the value of diverse events. Too often, they are skewed. It's likely that you have organised, or at least attended, a company event in the past. As an ally, you can help create diverse events that represent marginalised communities.

Be Transparent About the Pay Gap
Introducing transparency to promotion, pay and reward processes can reduce pay inequalities. Many allies share their salaries with female colleagues to ensure they aren't short-changed by their gender, especially if they have the same experience and potential.

Support Impartial Hiring Practices
The recruitment process itself, including the language, website and job description, should be gender neutral. As you identify your shortlist of qualified candidates, make sure to include more than one woman so the 'we don't have enough female candidates' excuse does not apply. Establishing objective criteria for reviewing resumés can help reduce bias, as does using structured interviews for recruitment and promotions. In the beginning of the process, interviewers should have a checklist describing biases and actionable advice to mitigate them.

Give Unbiased Appraisals
Women often get short-changed in reviews and miss out on critical talent assessment discussions. As an ally, you play a crucial role in removing bias when you or your team evaluate a woman's

performance. That is also an opportunity to ensure promotions are not skewed in favour of dominant groups.

Cater to Expectant Moms and New Mothers

Even if your company has few women employees, deliberate on incorporating a full range of policies to support pregnant women, including different types of leaves, parental leaves, lactation rooms and onsite mother rooms.

Extend Flexibility to Everyone

Pregnant or working mothers are not the only ones who need attention—everyone, including non-binary individuals, should be afforded respect and have the opportunity to thrive. Single and childless workers require policies that protect their needs too. These groups may have other care responsibilities or difficult situations that flexibility and support can help resolve.

Involve Key Stakeholders and Invest In Women-Focused Initiatives

Extend your goals and vision to your suppliers and customers, sharing your agenda with key stakeholders so they are inspired to follow suit. Share the steps you are taking to promote diversity on your end. If you can afford to, provide guidance to the local, national or global communities that you work with to build trust and long-term relationships. As an ally, you can also encourage your organisation to support employers and trade unions that represent female-dominated labour market sectors. If you are in a position to influence organisational spending on CSR projects, encourage leadership to consider redirecting women-owned business/micro business budgets to 'gender lens investing'—investing in products and services that benefit and empower women.

Stay the Course

It is important to recognise what stage your organisation is at in terms of gender equality and male allyship. Strike a balance between acknowledging the feelings of men who are reluctant to step up, while professionally and respectfully challenging resistant attitudes. Consider using The GROW Coaching Model or Benefit/Consequence Matrix. Share examples of how best-in-class companies and male role models are taking action to address gender equality and then encourage others to join the alliance.

SECTION FOUR

CHALLENGE THE INSTITUTION

'Throughout history, it has been the inaction of those who could have acted; the indifference of those who should have known better; the silence of the voice of justice when it mattered most; that has made it possible for evil to triumph.'
-Haile Selassie-

Now that you have successfully started challenging the policies and procedures in your own organisation, you are ready to advance to a macro level where you can champion activism that influences education, legislation and media. At this point you may be thinking, *how much more and how much longer? And how am I going to affect any change on that level?* I hear you. Not all of us can work on such a massive scale, but remember, there is strength in awareness and there is strength in numbers. The more aware you are of these bigger level challenges, the better position you will be in to create change, even if it's just by sharing your knowledge on a word of mouth level.

In the future, you may join an organisation that is in a powerful position to drive change on this kind of macro level. You could be reading this right now as a university student, but some day you could be a leader of your company. . . or even a country. Wherever your career takes you, consider how the following factors can impact gender equality and how you can potentially advance the cause.

SUPPORT EDUCATION

Giving girls access to quality education is crucial to realise a more equal world. Per UNICEF, most countries have achieved gender parity in primary enrolment, but in many countries, disparities persist. As an ally activist, you can help direct personal and organisational funds towards global education.

Insuring Women's Futures Impact Report 2021 by The Chartered Insurance Institute highlights the need for skills, qualification, career and financial guidance for girls and female students facing decisions during Covid-19 to help them make empowering choices to reach their academic and long-term career and economic potential. The report also recommends STEM and essential digital skills development opportunities and career guidance for mothers and older working women who have lost their jobs. Additionally, to encourage women to live a financially resilient life, it has been proposed that financial wellbeing for young people should be included as part of education systems. The report presses the need for formalising financial wellbeing activity and engaging young people on financial life journeys while embedding gender considerations to help improve financial capability (this involves supplementing numeracy, financial education on money management and finance facts within Personal, Social and Health Education (PSHE) classes).

Another way to positively impact education is to ensure a diverse curriculum particularly in terms of history—traditionally contributions and achievements of women and other under-represented groups have been sidelined and it's important to shine a spotlight on these untold stories.

Recent traumatising acts of systemic inequalities have uncovered the dire need to reflect full variety and diversity of British life and history, which takes it beyond the traditional focus. People are saying enough is enough and campaigning for much needed change.

Neville Gaunt, CEO of MindFit, recommends starting earlier with the youngest generation and formalising an education programme of cultural engagement, diversity and inclusion. Optimus Education suggests having open discussions and asking for feedback from Black, Asian, Multi-Ethnic colleagues, students and parents to understand their experiences. Even if it's uncomfortable, listen with compassion, be open to creating better systems for transparency and equality in the school community, decolonise the curriculum and familiarise staff with the Anti-Racism, Anti-Sexist Resource Lists. Books like the one you are reading, and others like it, can add value to the curriculum by making boys aware of how they can personally support their female counterparts.

I was recently invited to my son's school on International Women's Day to talk about how we can choose to challenge our own behaviour. The conversation sparked a healthy discussion and equality debates were initiated; the school also included many of the themes I had touched upon in their PSHE classes. This reaffirmed my firm belief in the power of dialogue that can set off awareness and push for meaningful change. As an ally and male role model, you too can speak up on issues that you care about. I hope this book has given you myriad ideas to get started.

One final step: consider serving on the board of educational institutes that help shape policy; here you can stand a stronger chance to advocate for much needed reforms.

CHAMPION INCLUSIVE GOVERNMENT POLICIES, LAWS AND REGULATIONS

'If you want to build a more equal country, you need to push equality for women into the political space,' says Sophie Walker, former leader of the Women's Equality Party. This essentially means supporting political agendas that prioritise women's equality.

Over the last century, global governments have introduced many progressive laws that support gender equality. Women can now own property on the same terms as men, serve on a jury, open a bank account and apply for a loan. In the UK, today we can sit in the House of Lords, work on the London Stock Exchange, secure a court order against an abusive spouse, get a legal abortion and report marital rape. If these rights are now possible, other rights can be too. Recently, Scotland became the first country in the world to make menstruation products free for all. There is now a legal duty on local authorities to ensure that free items such as tampons and sanitary pads are available to 'anyone who needs them'. The Bill was introduced by Labour MSP Monica Lennon who has been campaigning to end period poverty since 2016.

However, we still need to pass additional laws, particularly those that protect rape victims' rights and laws that make women feel safe and equal. The government has been especially urged to take immediate, concrete steps to give 'further reassurance' to women and girls in the wake of the killing of Sarah Everard, a 33-year-old Marketing Executive who went missing while walking home from a friend's house and whose body was later discovered in woodland in Kent, England. The government announced an additional £25 million for better lighting and CCTV, as well as a pilot scheme which would see plain-clothes officers in pubs and clubs. It also promised to bring in 'landmark legislation' to toughen up sentences and put more police on streets. However, demands for urgent action on issues such as harassment of women, domestic homicide sentencing and more support for victims of rape have yet to be addressed at the time of writing. The Police, Crime Sentencing and Courts Bill, which would change how protests are managed, including allowing police to impose conditions such as start and finish times, is still being debated and has been criticised as doing 'nothing to help women feel safer,' and imposing 'disproportionate' controls on freedom of speech.

Some antiquated laws need to be repealed as they no longer represent current norms. For example, an employer can still legally require female employees to wear high heels because the government rejected a law that would have banned this type of sexist behaviour in the workplace. Men, on the other hand, must dress with an 'equivalent level of smartness.' Thanks to Gina Martin's powerful rallies and support, 'up skirting' is now officially a criminal offence but we have a long way to go in terms of other measures.

The gender data gap mentioned earlier is another persistent problem. 'The lack of data makes it difficult to set policies and gauge progress, preventing governments and organisations from taking measurable steps to empower women and improve lives,' says Mayra Buvinic, a UN Foundation senior fellow working on Data2X, an initiative aimed at closing the gender data gap. 'Not having data on a certain area, behaviour or society means that you cannot design the right policies, you cannot track progress, you cannot evaluate,' she says. 'You are basically not accountable.'

'Data alone, however, doesn't set policy,' says Buvinic of Data2X. 'We have to get politicians and countries designing programs based on data,' she says. 'There's no point in generating all this new data if it's not going to be used.'

In her book, *Invisible Women*, author and activist Caroline Criado Perez recognises how important it is to close this gender data gap. She notes, 'human history is comprised of a pervasive gender data gap that effectively "silences" and erases women's accomplishments, experiences, needs and daily lives.' Her book reveals that there is a frightening amount we don't know about women. She writes, 'From medical research to car safety to economic statistics, the vast majority of the world's data is based on men—male bodies and male lives. The result is that medication is less likely to work for women and is more likely to cause (more severe) adverse reactions.' Transportation systems, medical devices and treatments, tax structures, consumer products, even the smartphones and voice-recognition technologies we use every day have been designed with less consideration for women. All of this is a consequence of a global mentality that considers humanity as almost exclusively male.

We can address this data gap by creating a more integrated approach to inclusive, evidence-based decision-making and ensuring data collection is sex-disaggregated to identify the discrimination. The Women's Equalities Committee recommends that data not only be collected and published disaggregated by sex but also other protected characteristics in a way that 'facilitates reporting and analysis on how, for example, gender, ethnicity, disability, age and socio-economic status interact, and can compound, disadvantage.' If you work for an organisation that collects this type of data, press for data parity and ask the right questions to brings diversity into the process.

In addition, we need to work together to reduce bias in collection algorithms. Artificial Intelligence systems learn to make decisions based on training data, which can include biased human decisions or reflect historical or social inequities, even if sensitive variables such as gender, race, or sexual orientation are removed.

In 2020, a group of female MPs from the UK's Liberal Democrat Party were seeking to drive change by tabling Bills that would establish laws against inequality. In her article *Seven Gaps in the Law that Are Still Totally Screwing Women Over*, author Catriona Harvey-Jenner reveals how we can replace antiquated existing laws with relevant ones for today's society:

- A Bill that requires schools to let pupils use the toilet during lesson time.
- A Bill that gives women offenders community sentences unless they have committed a serious or violent offence and pose a threat to the public.
- A Bill requiring the government to report on the impact of UK aid in tackling period poverty.
- A Bill to prohibit the gender price gap/pink tax.
- A Bill to make misogyny a hate crime.
- A Bill to make support services for victims of sexual, violent and domestic abuse a right.
- A Bill to prohibit anti-abortion protests within 150 metres of abortion clinics.

After the dreadful killing of Sarah Everard, the issue of violence against women and girls has been at the forefront and several figures from across the political spectrum have offered proposals to tackle the ongoing blight. One well-received proposal labels misogyny as a hate crime. Police forces across England and Wales will identify these crimes as such when a victim believes a crime has been prompted by 'hostility based on their sex.' Home Office minister Baroness Williams said that the data would initially be gathered 'on an experimental basis,' pending recommendations for a longer-term solution from the Law Commission which has conducted a review of hate crime legislation.

Stella Creasy, MP for Walthamstow who led the campaign, said, 'It will be taken into account in the sentencing in court in the same way that it is if someone is being targeted because of the colour of their skin.' However, equality campaigners argue this will not make much difference given cases rarely get that far.

In 2016, Nottingham Police Force introduced a new misogyny hate crime policy in the city. Yet over a two-year period, only 174 women reported misogyny hate crimes, with only 101 recorded as hate crimes and just one resulting in a conviction. An analysis of the policy by the University of Nottingham and Nottingham Trent University found that the institutionalised hurdles and cultural barriers within the very police force enacting the policy need to be addressed too—many of these custodians of safety still lack clarity of power dynamics and what constitutes misogyny. Very often we hear of police officials engaging in victim blaming and attributing crimes to unsafe choices made by women. All in all, it is essential to invest in preventative and interventionist strategies that also involve shaping men's perceptions and helping them identify misogynistic behaviour. This effort begins in schools and homes.

Pro-women laws ensure future economies will be dynamic and inclusive, offering equal opportunity to everyone. Even if you are not in a government position, you can still lobby for such laws, write letters and sign petitions just like other activists do. Even small actions count and can potentially make a huge difference. Your one step forward could possibly inspire several others to do the same. However, creating meaningful laws is as important as enforcing them. Otherwise, the battle for women's rights is only half won.

CALL OUT MEDIA BIAS

Media is perhaps the most pervasive and powerful influence amongst the plethora of influences that shape our gender views. Media is ever-present, ingrained in the very fabric of our society. It is nearly impossible to avoid and its never-ending stream of messages permeates our consciousness at every turn.

Through television, newspapers and magazines, music videos, video games and every other form of entertainment, the media bombards us with gender stereotyping that has helped form our societal norms. *The Influence of Media on Views of Gender* by Julia T. Wood highlights how all forms of media communicate images of the sexes, many of which perpetuate unrealistic, stereotypical, and limiting perceptions.

There are predominantly three themes that represent gender in media. First and foremost is the under-representation of women, which connects to the broader historical and cultural narrative where men are the universal norm and thus women are less visible and insignificant. Secondly, men and women are depicted in stereotypical ways that reflect and reinforce socially endorsed views of gender. Thirdly, the portrayal of male and female relationships highlights traditional roles that only help normalise gender violence against women.

The report notes: 'Typically, men are portrayed as active, adventurous, powerful, sexually aggressive and largely uninvolved in human relationships. Just as consistent with cultural views of gender are depictions of women as sex objects who are usually young, thin, beautiful, passive, dependent, and often incompetent and dumb. Female characters devote their primary energies to improving their appearances and taking care of homes and people. Because media pervade our lives, the ways they misrepresent genders may distort how we see ourselves and what we perceive as normal and desirable for men and women.'

In the two years since I called attention to this issue in my first book, the UK's advertising watchdog group introduced a ban on adverts featuring 'harmful gender stereotypes' or those which are likely to cause 'serious or widespread offence.' The group discovered that some portrayals could play a part in 'limiting people's potential.' The new rule follows a review of gender stereotyping in adverts by the Advertising Standards Authority (ASA)—the organisation that administers the UK Advertising Codes, which covers both broadcast and non-broadcast adverts, including online and social media. The review revealed that harmful stereotypes could 'restrict the choices, aspirations and opportunities of children, young people and adults and these stereotypes can be reinforced by some advertising, which plays a part in unequal gender outcomes.'

'Our evidence shows how harmful gender stereotypes in ads can contribute to inequality in society, with costs for all of us. Put simply, we found that some portrayals in ads can, over time, play a part in limiting people's potential,' said ASA chief executive Guy Parker.

Other situations likely to fall foul of the new rule include:

- Adverts that show a man or a woman failing at a task because of their gender, such as a man failing to change a nappy or a woman failing to park a car.
- Adverts aimed at new mothers suggesting that looking good or keeping a home tidy is more important than emotional wellbeing.
- Adverts which belittle a man for carrying out stereo-typically female roles. However, the new rules do not

preclude the use of all gender stereotypes. The ASA said the aim was to identify 'specific harms' that should be prevented.

Even though films and dramas now feature women in leading roles—even women as superheroes—that does not outweigh the more pervasive 'women as eye candy' casting, according to a new study that found 'harmful stereotypes' still dominate the big screen.

Oscar-winning star of *Thelma and Louise,* Geena Davis has also created the Geena Davis Institute on Gender in Media that aims to address harmful gender stereotypes. She believes that girls need to see themselves reflected on screen through 'positive and authentic characters who inspire them.' She adds, 'Content creators and storytellers in entertainment and media have an opportunity to support and influence the aspirations of girls and women and stop reinforcing damaging gender stereotypes.'

As an ally, you can play a role in highlighting these incongruities. Social media is a valuable tool to extend the impact and reach of our message; and it's free. Challenge and counteract media that intentionally or unintentionally undermines women's rights; make your voice heard by raising your concerns and registering your complaints where appropriate. Men are now actively engaging in open conversations across social media by challenging the status quo, questioning harmful norms, calling out sexist comments or acts, tweeting hashtags, writing articles, and sharing videos and podcasts to show their solidarity for equality campaigns. Men who make their voices heard are a welcome addition in spaces where women have been fighting on their own for a long time. They are now truly interested in becoming part of the solution, whether it is because of the women in their lives (partners, sisters and daughters) or given increased awareness of equality challenges and benefits. Many leading celebrities and politicians have joined the fight and are lobbying for change too. As women, we couldn't be more grateful.

SUMMARY

Support Education

As an ally activist, you can help direct personal and organisational funds towards global education. You can also push for formalising financial wellbeing education for young girls to help improve financial capability and futures considerations. Another way to positively impact education is to ensure a diverse curriculum, particularly in terms of history. Traditionally, contributions and achievements of women and other under-represented groups have been sidelined and it's important to shine a spotlight on these untold stories. One final step: consider serving on the board of educational institutes that help shape policy and can advocate for these much needed changes.

Champion Inclusive Government Policies, Laws and Regulations

Pro-women laws ensure future economies will be dynamic and inclusive, offering equal opportunity to everyone. Even if you do not hold a government position, you can still lobby for such laws, write letters and sign petitions as other activists do. Even small actions have value and can potentially make a huge difference. Your one step forward could possibly inspire several others to do the same. However, creating meaningful laws is as important as enforcing them.

Call Out Media Bias

Media is perhaps the most pervasive and powerful influence amongst the myriad influences that shape our gender views. Television, newspapers and magazines, music videos, video games and every other form of entertainment bombard us with gender stereotyping that has helped form our societal norms. As an ally, you can play a role in highlighting these incongruities. Social media is a valuable tool to extend the impact and reach of our message; what's more, it's free. Challenge and counteract media that intentionally or unintentionally undermines women's rights; make your voice heard by raising your concerns and registering your complaints where appropriate.

CLOSING THOUGHTS

'We will never truly unlock or open opportunities for women, young or old, unless we change the mindset of every social structure, family, and community. How? Well, it can't be just women who speak up for women. So, it's our responsibility as men to not only talk the talk, but walk it as well.'
-Jay Andrews-

You now have the strategies you need to develop into a powerful advocate for women. But allyship is not easy. It requires patience, practice, motivation and momentum. Whenever you try anything new that bucks traditional norms it can be frightening, especially if you receive pushback. The first step toward managing this is self-awareness; it is key to changing mindset and behaviour. You will probably not like the disruption at first, but you will adapt. Setbacks are inevitable, and you will make mistakes, but as long as you learn from them they should not be a source of shame and embarrassment. Remind yourself to have realistic expectations. You will never be the perfect ally—no one is—not even the most seasoned champion. The fact that you are reading this book means you are committed to the journey.

Know that the journey might be exhausting at times, especially since the pandemic continues to overturn our lifestyles and routines. In these challenging times, it's difficult to fight your own battles, let alone someone else's. However, this is exactly when your intervention will matter most. Covid-19 is magnifying gender-based inequalities around the world, reversing decades of progress towards equality and sustainable development goals. We have made significant progress in the fight toward equality and we cannot afford to lose momentum. Losing ground at this stage will have dire consequences for women, especially when we have come this far. It's imperative that women, girls, and other vulnerable groups receive focused attention from the global community.

The events of 2020 turned workplaces, education and childcare upside down. Certain ethnicities are already coping with the disproportionate impact of Covid-19. The *McKinsey & Company LeanIn Women in the Workplace 2020 Report* revealed, 'as a result of these dynamics, more than one in four women are contemplating what many would have considered unthinkable just six months ago: downshifting their careers or leaving the workforce completely. Companies risk losing women in leadership—and future women leaders—and unwinding years of painstaking progress toward gender diversity.' According to the report, 'Corporate America' is at a critical crossroads—and the UK faces a similar juncture. However, the crisis presents hope and opportunity if companies make large-scale investments to create flexible and empathetic work place environments—many have already started doing so.

Your allyship can make a difference today and in future days, even if that progress is achieved one small win at a time. You have the chance to help lay the foundation for a more flexible and equitable workplace of tomorrow. You have the opportunity to positively impact your partners, friends and other women in your circle by helping them achieve their potential. Collectively, we all have the opportunity to lay the groundwork for future generations, generations that will include our children and grandchildren.

As you progress on this journey, be mindful that some men will be reluctant to embrace diverse values and inclusivity. You won't be able to convert everyone to the cause. Be respectful of differing opinions, but ensure everyone offers that same level of respect to others through their communication and behaviour.

How well this allyship serves you and the people you hope to influence depends on how deeply you integrate these strategies into your day-to-day life. You may want to solicit fellow allies for your journey and demonstrate public commitment. The truth of the matter is that we are tired of fighting alone, but with you on our side we can change the narrative and rewrite the story.

As an ally, you are the missing piece of the gender equality puzzle. Women need your support to affect positive change for women of every colour and race, in every community and profession. As an ally, you can help inspire others to stand up and be bold. As an ally, you can help remove the roadblocks we women face in our personal and professional lives—roadblocks that are only in place because of our gender. As an ally, your mentorship can help us navigate overwhelming self-doubt. As an ally, even your smallest act of activism can be powerful enough to erode ingrained stereotypes. As an ally, you can convert good intention into positive action. As an ally, you can lead through advocacy and serve as a role model for other men.

And as women, we recognise and value the support of men like you: allies like you. You inspire us. You empower us. You make us want to achieve more, and be more, because you believe in our potential. So, on behalf of women around the world, please accept our sincere gratitude for being *that kind* of man, because it is exactly the *right kind* of man we all need to finally achieve gender equality.

ABOUT THE AUTHOR

An inspiring leadership trainer and career coach, Hira Ali has been committed to helping others achieve their inherent potential throughout her award-winning career. She is an Associate Certified Coach accredited by the International Coaching Federation (ICF) and a licensed Neuro Linguistic Programming (NLP) Practitioner. Hira is also a successful entrepreneur who has launched several businesses to support her mission including Advancing Your Potential, Career Excel, International Women Empowerment Events and most recently, The Grey Area, which focuses on *decoding inclusion*. Her work has been featured in *Forbes, Huff Post,* and *Entrepreneur*, among hundreds of other print, radio and television outlets, and has earned Hira several prestigious honours including the *Top 100 Women-Lift Effects* award, the *Women in Media* award, and recognition as a top three finalist for The Baton Awards *Entrepreneur of the Year*. She was recently appointed as The Senior Advisory Team member at The Benedictine University Illinois L.E.A.D.S leadership program for undergraduate women.

Hira was also included in a list by DiverseIn of global D&I voices to follow on LinkedIn. In addition, she has been featured as a role model in the book *Girls Who Do You Want To Be* alongside phenomenal world changers. Hira is passionate about empowering women and ethnic minorities, closing the gender gap and advocating diversity and inclusion in the workplace. Her wealth of positive client testimonials underscores her commitment to helping others realise their goals and achieve their potential.

In 2019, Hira released her first book entitled *Her Way To The Top: A Guide to Smashing the Glass Ceiling* which received outstanding testimonials worldwide. Hira's second companion book—*Her Allies:*

A Practical Toolkit to Help Men Lead Through Advocacy—invites men to join the gender equality movement.

For more on Hira, please visit www.advancingyourpotential.com.

You can follow Hira's work here:
Twitter: @advancingyou
Instagram: @advancingyou
Facebook: @advancingyou
LinkedIn: @advancingyou @HiraAli Coach

OTHER WAYS TO MAKE A DIFFERENCE

There are other more immediate ways you can make a difference too. Consider joining our campaign at iweevents.com using the hashtags #HerAllies, #ChallengingMyself, #ChallengingOthers #ChallengingTheOrganisationalCulture and #ChallengingTheInstitution. Don't forget to tag us too!

Advancing Your Potential

Advancing Your Potential offers customised workshops and webinars on Team Management, Mental Health and Wellbeing, Race & Ethnicity, Women's Leadership and Allyship. Our interactive leadership workshops are backed by principles of psychology and neuroscience and our content integrates decades of international coaching, training and professional experience with the latest research. Additionally, we offer Executive Coaching, Surveys, Polls and Benchmarking, Focus Groups and D&I consultancy. At Advancing Your Potential, we specialise in designing business solutions specifically targeted towards organisational needs. For years, our team has helped organisations create diverse and collaborative cultures that fuel innovation; we believe that inclusive companies consistently beat homogenous ones when it comes to revenue, profitability, and decision-making.

www.advancingyourpotential.com @advancingyou

Career Excel

Career Excel offers the most comprehensive online leadership training program available to help women achieve their professional potential through live coaching, global networking and an in-depth curriculum.

www.careerexcel.us @careerexcelcrew

The Grey Area
The Grey Area offers customised surveys and reports designed to capture the experience of multi-ethnic men and women working in the public and private sector followed by in-depth comprehensive reports and analysis.
www.thegreyarea.uk @tgaInclusion

International Women Empowerment Events
IWEE aims to be seen as trusted voice for women empowerment in Asia. We collaborate with inspirational leaders and influencers locally and internationally to bring awareness of the underlying root causes impacting women's empowerment throughout Asia and the Middle East—causes that have negatively impacted women from achieving equality in health, education, work and politics.
www.iweeglobal.com @iweeglobal

REFERENCES

Her Way To The Top: A guide to smashing the glass ceiling
Hira Ali

Are you biased? I am
TEDxBasel by Kristen Pressner

Sexism in publishing: 'My novel wasn't the problem, it was me, Catherine'
Alison Flood

Her Way To The Top Book Launch Anniversary
Welum, Lizet Esquivel

How to Overcome Our Biases; Walk Bolding towards Them
TEDxBeaconStreet by Vernā Myers

Better Allies
Karen Catlin

Reasons Why So Many People Believe Feminism Hates Men and Why They're Not True
Sam Killerman

Good Guys
David G Smith, W. Brad Johnson

Both Men and Women Have To Address Gender Inequality
British Council

Tempered Radicals as Institutional Change Agents: The Case of Advancing Gender Equity at the University of Michigan
Debra E. Meyerson, Megan Tompkins-Stange

Why Men Are Winning at Work
Gill Whitty-Collins

References

Better Allies
Karen Catlin

Five Ways Men Can Improve Gender Diversity at Work
Matt Krentz, Olivier Wierzba, Katie Abouzahr, Jennifer Garcia-Alonso
and Frances Brooks Taplett

Men as Allies: Engaging Men to Advance Women in the Workplace
A curated research report by Centre for Women and Business at
Bentley University

Emma Watson: Gender equality is your issue too
UN Women

Five Ways Men Can Improve Gender Diversity at Work
Matt Krentz, Olivier Wierzba, Katie Abouzahr, Jennifer Garcia-Alonso,
and Frances Brooks Taplett

Americans Crave a New Kind of Leader—and Women Are Ready to Deliver
BNY Mellon's Pershing online study commissioned to Harris Poll

*Rethink What You 'Know' About High-Achieving Women: A Survey of
Harvard Business School Graduates Sheds New Light on What Happens
to Women—and Men—After Business School*
Robin J. Ely, Pamela Stone, and Colleen Ammerman

*Men Now Avoid Women at Work—Another Sign We're Being Punished
For #MeToo*
Arwa Mahdawi

Engaging Men in Gender Initiatives: What Change Agents Need To Know
Catalyst

*Research by The Gloria Cordes Larson Center for Women and Business
(CWB)*
Bentley University

Six Ways to Taking Feminism Back
Huff Post, Hira Ali

Reactions to Gender Egalitarian Men: Perceived Feminisation Due To Stigma-By-Association
Laurie A. Rudman, Kris Mescher, Corinne A. Moss-Racusin

How Men Can Become Better Allies to Women
Harvard Business Review, W. Brad Johnson, David G. Smith

The Pedestal Effect: Problems and Potentiality for Feminist Men
Peretz, Tal H

Liberating the 'Men's Men' In Our Midst
Terry Howard

How to lead like an Ally
Julie Kratz

Women in the Workplace
McKinsey & Company

Working Together: Diversity as Opportunity
Angeles Arrien, Mikhail Sergeevich Gorbachev

Internal and External Challenges Faced By Women And Ethnic Minorities That Make Them More Vulnerable At Work
Forbes, Hira Ali

Why Presenteeism Is Bad Business Practice
Working Mums, Hira Ali

To Hold Women Back, Keep Treating Them Like Men
Harvard Business Review, Avivah Wittenberg-Cox

Unleash the Power of the Female Brain
Dr Daniel Amen

References

Women Have More Active Brains Than Men, According to Science
World Economic Forum, Rosamond Hutt

How Women Can Succeed in the Workplace
Stanford Business School, Marguerite Rigoglioso

The Confidence Code the Science and Art of Self-Assurance—What Women Should Know
Katty Kay, Claire Shipman

The Minority Stress Perspective
Michael P. Dentato, PhD, MSW

Equality for Girls—Girls' Attitudes Survey 2013
Girl Guiding

A New Look at Adolescent Girls
American Psychological Association's (APA's) Presidential Task Force on Adolescent Girls: Strengths and Stresses, Dorothy W. Cantor. Institute of Leadership and Management Ambition and Gender at Work

Why Women Don't Ask: The High Cost of Avoiding Negotiation, and Positive Strategies for Change
Linda Babcock, Sara Laschever

Strengthening Young Women's Leadership
UN Women

In Focus: 16 Days of Activism against Gender-based Violence
UN Women

Gender-Based Violence in the Workplace
Human Rights Watch

Benevolent Sexism: A Feminist Comic Explains How It Holds Women Back
The Guardian, Emma

Women Vs Capitalism
Vicky Pryce

The State of the Gender Pay Gap in 2021
PayScale

Melinda Gates Offers a Solution to Time Poverty
Time, Kirsten Salyer

What Women Can't Let Go; Real Simple
Julia Edelstein

Five Ways the Coronavirus is Adversely Impacting Women
Ellevate, Hira Ali

How Women are Getting Squeezed by The Pandemic
The New York Times, Francesca Donner

Gender Inequality in Research Productivity During the Covid-19 Pandemic
Ruomeng Cui Goizueta Business School, Emory University, ruomeng.cui@emory.edu, Hao Ding Goizueta Business School, Emory University, hao.ding@emory.edu, Feng Zhu Harvard Business School, Harvard University, fzhu@hbs.edu

Overcoming the 'Tyranny of the Urgent': Integrating Gender into Disease Outbreak Preparedness And Response
Julia Smith

Women Still Less Likely To Be Active in the Labour Market than Men in Most of The World
ILO

Why Women May Face a Greater Risk of Catching Coronavirus
The New York Times, Alisha Haridasani Gupta

Pregnant Then Screwed: The Truth About the Motherhood Penalty
Joeli Brearley

References

The 90% Economy That Lockdowns Will Leave Behind. Not Quite All There
The Economist

Addressing Sex and Gender In Epidemic-Prone Infectious Diseases
World Health Organisation

Gender Equity In The Health Workforce: Analysis Of 104 Countries
Mathieu Boniol, Michelle McIsaac, Lihui Xu, Tana Wuliji, Khassoum Diallo, Jim Campbell

The Perspective of Gender on the Ebola Virus Using a Risk Management and Population Health Framework: A Scoping Review
Miriam N. Nkangu, Oluwasayo A. Olatunde, and Sanni Yaya

Diaries from the Field is the Powerful Nurse-Led Movement That We All Need to Get Behind Right Now
Marie Claire, Jenny Proudfoot

TrustRadius 2021 Women in Tech Report
Trust Radius

Sexism on the Covid-19 Frontline: 'PPE is Made for a 6ft 3in Rugby Player'
The Guardian, Alexandra Topping

Women Shoulder Most of the Extra Work Because of Covid-19
Thomson Reuters Foundation New, Rachel Thomas

Why Women May Face a Greater Risk of Catching Coronavirus
The New York Times, Alisha Haridasani Gupta

Checklist for Covid-19 Response
UN Women Deputy Executive Director, Åsa Regnér

Unequal Impact? Coronavirus and the Gendered Economic Impact
Report by House of Commons Women and Equalities Committee

The Grey Area survey
www.thegreyarea.uk

Women's Coverage, Access, and Affordability: Key Findings from the 2017 Kaiser Women's Health Survey
Usha Ranji, Caroline Rosenzweig, and Alina Salganicoff of the Kaiser Family Foundation

Shaved Heads, Adult Diapers: Life as a Nurse in the Coronavirus Outbreak
The New York Times, Alexandra Stevenson

Engaging Men in Gender Initiatives: What Change Agents Need To Know
Catalyst

Caroline Criado Perez: How I Put a Suffragist in Parliament
The Guardian, Nicci Gerrard

Crucial Conversations Tools for Talking When Stakes Are High, Second Edition
Kerry Patterson , Joseph Grenny, Ron McMillan, Al Switzler

How to Be More Empathetic During Crises
Executive Secretary Magazine, Hira Ali

Demarginalising the Intersection of Race and Sex: A Black Feminist Critique of Antidiscrimination Doctrine, Feminist Theory and Antiracist Politics
Kimberle Crenshaw

Mary Maxfield
https://www.marymaxfield.com/

Quietly Visible: Leading with Influence and Impact as an Introverted Woman
Carol Stewart

Guidelines for Gender-Inclusive Language in English
UN Women

Catalyst Bias Correct
National Center for Transgender Equality

Understanding Non-Binary People: How to Be Respectful and Supportive
National Center for Transgender Equality

References

How to Overcome Our Biases; Walk Bolding Towards Them
TEDxBeaconStreet, Vernā Myers

The Incredible Power of Staff Networks
Cherron Inko-Tariah MBE

Seven Ways Men Can Support Women as Allies;
Forbes, Hira Ali

The Awakened Family: How to Raise Empowered, Resilient, and Conscious Children.
Dr Shefali Tsabary

Eight Ways You Can Support Racially Diverse Colleagues At Your Workplace
Forbes, Hira Ali

The Common Habit That Undermines Organisations' Diversity Efforts
Fast Company, Dr Suzanne Wertheim

Ten Ways We Can Support Women in the Workplace During A Crisis
Forbes, Hira Ali

To Reach True Gender Equality We Must Focus On Good Male Role Models
Metro UK , June Sarpong

Let Her Fly: A Father's Journey and the Fight for Equality
Ziauddin Yousafzai, Louise Carpenter

Ten Career Tips for Every Working Woman
Forbes, Hira Ali

Four Easy and Effective Steps to Support the International Women's Day 2020 'Each for Equal Theme'
Forbes, Hira Ali

How Women are Stepping Up to Remake Rwanda
Rania Abouzeid

'Mothers are livid. We've had enough!' The Pregnant Women Being Forced Out of the Workplace
Emine Saner

All In: How Our Work-First Culture Fails Dads, Families, and Businesses-And How We Can Fix It Together
Josh Levs

Women of Colour Get Asked to Do More 'Office Housework;' Here's How They Can Say No
Ruchika Tulshyan

Boys Won't Be Boys, Boys Will Be What We Teach Them To Be
TEDxLondonWomen, Ben Hurst

Managing Remote Teams: How to Keep it Effective and Personal
Thrive Global, Hira Ali

How to Lead Like an Ally
Julie Kratz

Gender Bias at Work Turns Up in Feedback
Wall Street Journal, Rachel Emma Silverman

Fans Are Calling Keanu Reeves A 'Respectful King' After Noticing He Doesn't Touch Women In Photos
Insider, Callie Ahlgrim

The Unconscious Rules of Personal Space: The Distance You Keep From Others is an Elaborate, Instinctive Dance
Michael Graziano

Think Twice Before Hiring Your Leaders: Their Values Dictate Your Brand
Ellevate Network, Cindy Wahler

Gender, Attitudes Towards Women, and the Appreciation Of Sexist Humour
Timothy E. Moore, Karen Griffiths and Barbara Payne

What Did He Mean By That? Humour Decreases Attributions of Sexism and Confrontation of Sexist Jokes
Robyn K. Mallett, Thomas E. Ford and Julie A. Woodzicka

Locker Room Talk Isn't Harmless; It Normalises Rape
The Guardian, Jaclyn Friedman

My Boss Sexually Harassed Me At The Work Christmas Party. What Should I Do?
Louisa Symington-Mills

Sarah Everard Murder Highlights Threats Faced by Minority Women
AlJazeera, Anu Shukla

A Researcher Asked Men and Women To List Things To Avoid Sexual Assault, The Answers Are Shocking
KC Archna

Men Now Avoid Women at Work – Another Sign We're Being Punished For #MeToo
Arwa Mahdawi

Sexual Harassment in the Workplace Defined
Rebecca Berlin

Examples of Sexual Harassment
Alison Doyle

EU Commission Code of Practice on Measures to Combat Sexual Harassment
Slater and Gordon Lawyers, UK Press Release

Workplace Harassment – What It is and What to Do About It
Velsoft

Not All Men, But Still Too Many Men
TerribleMinds

From 'Not All Men' to 'Men Are\ Victims Too', Things Not to Say When Women Talk About Sexual Harassment
Firstpost, Sian Lewis

Sexual Consent Really Isn't Like a Cup of Tea – But at Least We're Talking About It
Laura Hood

Why Sexual Consent Is Just like Offering Someone a Cup of Tea It really is this simple
Jo Barrow, Emmeline May, Sian Butcher

Everyone's Invited
https://www.everyonesinvited.uk/

How Everyone's Invited's 'rape culture' claims sparked a #MeToo movement in UK schools
Evening Standard, Katie Strick

Six Simple, Effective Ways to Take Back Feminism
Hira Ali

A Step By Step Process for Self-Coaching Yourself towards Productivity and Success
Hira Ali

The Simple Trick Women in the White House Use to Stop Getting Interrupted
Alyse Kalish

Six Steps For Handling Gender-Based Psychological Violence At The Workplace
Forbes, Hira Ali

TrustRadius 2020 Women in Tech Report
Trust Radius

How L&D Managers Can Lead a Valuable Risk Management Program
Training Industry, Hira Ali

References

Does Working From Home Save Companies Money?
Baruch Silvermann

Gendered Media: The Influence of Media on Views of Gender
Julia T. Wood

Ten Ways We Can Support Women in the Workplace during A Crisis
Forbes, Hira Ali

Two in Five Working Mums Face Childcare Crisis When New Term Starts
TUC poll

Childcare Crisis Risks Pushing Women Out of Workforce
Alexandra Topping

Five Strategies For Narrowing the Gender Pay Gap
Forbes, Hira Ali

The Five Biggest Biases That Affect Decision-Making
Chris Weller

One Way to Reduce Gender Bias in Performance Reviews
Lauren Rivera and András Tilcsik

How Gender Bias Corrupts Performance Reviews, and What to Do About It
Paola Cecchi-Dimeglio

The GROW Model: The practical coaching model driven by a powerful coaching philosophy
Performance Consulting

Closing the Gender Data Gap: How Efforts to Collect Data about Women and Girls Drive Global Economic and Social Progress
The New York Times

Harmful Gender Stereotypes in Adverts Banned
BBC

Invisible Women: Exposing Data Bias in a World Designed for Men
Caroline Criado Perez

Unequal impact? Coronavirus and the gendered economic impact
Report by House of Commons Women and Equalities Committee

Women in the Workplace: Corporate America is at a Critical Crossroads
McKinsey & Company, LeanInDolectum ea quis ipsapis int lam
iusam int es verionsed quam ex ex eos quias utemquae. Ur reicaecte
namusanti dellaborerum qui dolest, estotatem iniasiti rerunt dest,
volum qui bero dem hictur, occupta taturio rporpor mint dolo esti
blab ipicimus, inihillanda et etur, quam, sapelique nem aut vel ium
aut ut litio. Itatio. Nam et adigent eritae. Nist, sam evelluptatem
quibus inctia doluptia nim accae pe sitem accae eos diore volore aut
adi dolor mintiustrum ilique et ent maximil landis et harum venitia
doluptat a volorion et unt.

Hit quo core aspedi aut veror auda sita aut ex everumque volupta
taspide explate laboremped excepe dolor rerum qui quam nonsequia
que es in net aliqui ulpa dit qui beatur alibusa pidenti oresseq uiatur
sequiamus conse nessitas dolupta di sitatus etur sitas et eventiunt.

Tur? Quia dictio. Nemque quo omni dollibus et enis dicae etum
facim quis qui dolest aligendus.

Piderro quis renissunt, alibus.

Rovitiam es milia a sus et verit et elendanit aut ma dias asperia
ipsanih iliquunt.

Maionsent que mil ipis poratqu atectatiam ex es dolest, et hicid eumet
voluptate reius modit pos arum explisita eum sit, sequuntur, corernam
quis est, omnis explacil idite pa endandeles quis molorumque
digendignis non pe nonsed qui optatur, sundipsam entur as doluptas
duntiatem harum, siminis magnimus simus dest volo tecab imus
denem et omnimet mi, ut magniaspe lania poreper roviderempor
samenim quamend untiatur? Tem. Ariaecuptam, sae prent facienda
expliquodios volorem est unt volectiost apienec taturia vel maiorro
quosam, velitat enderepudit, idis dusaper ibeaquam dolore nossi
voluptia aut explibe rumquam reium quis delest facerisim vendi
sumet quat.

Luptatendis simusti ssintem quiatum delique natem volenti scitate